Praise for Fix
Financial Free

"I've purchased several of Mark's books. By far his books and other resources should be at the top of the list for those who are seeking the real deal in learning about real estate investing. With so much overhyped and unrealistic investing information available, by far Mark is one of the best. He's the best because he walks the walk and talks the talk. He's a practicing agent, built real estate sales and investing teams and is truly authentic in communicating his successes and failures or learning experiences.

I highly recommend his books. I've paid twice or more for some other books and received significantly less than the content in Mark's books." -HUDPRO

"I just wanted to take the time to thank you for the 30-minute phone call on Friday, March 4th. I have my first deal under contract, DUE TO YOUR SUGGESTIONS, all cash offer, no contingencies on a Short Sale. We should close sometime this month. We got the home for $105,000 and will put $35,000 in, and it will be a $227,000 house. We plan on keeping it for a rental. This deal would not have been possible without your advice. Keep up the GREAT work! Thanks so much!" -Kim Martin

"I am working my way through Mark's books and have just finished this one. A ton of great information and good advice on avoiding trouble. I highly recommend this book for anyone considering this investing approach." -Ray Lang

"An outstanding book on real life fixing and flipping Real Estate investing from what has become a trusted source for me. Easy to read and no-nonsense including problem deals and what to expect in this facet of REI. Looking forward to more from Mark and appreciate his efforts to pass along knowledge and accelerate the learning/success curve." -James

"This book has detailed all the know-hows and is very informative. Mark's blog also provides a very good source of information on financing investment properties, and how to look at investment property deals. A must read if you're serious about making moves in the real estate business." -Xing Gao

"This book is a GREAT way to learn how to make money in real estate. If you are really serious about making money in real estate you absolutely must get this book. Mark Ferguson has truly invested in this great book to show us how to make money. This is not a get rich quick scheme but you can, if you are willing to do the work. You will learn all about finding the deals, performing analysis, finding contractors, making repairs, selling for profit and managing multiple properties. Thanks Mark for sharing this information with us." -Katina

Fix and Flip Your Way to Financial Freedom

Finding, Financing, Repairing, and Selling Investment Properties.

Mark Ferguson

InvestFourMore.com

ASIN: B00M8LEZWI

Cover Design: Pixel Sudio

Interior Design: Justin Gesso

Editing: Gregory Alan Helmerick

Printed in the USA

The information presented herein represents the views of the author as of the date of the publication. This book is presented for informational purposes only. Due to the rate at which conditions change, the author reserves the right to alter and update his opinions based on new conditions. While every attempt has been made to verify the information in this book, neither the author nor his affiliates/partners assume any responsibility for errors, inaccuracies, or omissions.

Table of Contents

6

Dedication

Thank you to my wonderful wife, Jeni, who puts up with my flipping. Sometimes, I buy a few too many houses at once that need a little too much work, but it has always worked in the end, and I could not do this without her trust.

Special Bonus and Investing Tools

I love flipping houses, and in 2017, I am still a very active flipper. I have had from 15 to 20 flips going at once the entire year. If you want to see what is going on with me, check out my blog: InvestFourMore.com.

I have many free resources on my website, including a weekly podcast, new articles each week, and much more.

To help others learn real estate investing, I have written books and created coaching programs that include personal help from me. My programs are not ultra-expensive like most flipping courses. I make them affordable in order to reach as many people as possible.

To learn more about what I have to offer, check out this page and get your special discount code.

https://investfourmore.com/bonus

Introduction

Fixing and flipping houses can be a fantastic business that generates a lot of income. However, flipping is not a get-rich-quick business and is not easy by any means. I have been fixing and flipping houses since 2001, and I have fix and flipped over 120 houses in that time. I have flipped in a seller's market, a buyer's market, and everything in between. As I write this book (updated in 2017), much of the country is in a very hot seller's market. Many people think it is impossible to flip in this environment, but I am flipping more houses than I ever have before. A great fix and flipper should be able to buy houses and make money in any market.

I try to make at least $25,000 on each fix and flip, and I average over $30,000 in profit on the flips I complete. I flipped 12 houses in 2014, 8 in 2015, 17 in 2016, and plan to flip 30 in 2017. In this book, I will discuss the details involved with flipping, including how to buy, finance, and repair properties, how to find contractors. I also provide detailed information on my fix and flips, and discuss how I flip up to 20 houses at once.

Flipping is nothing like they make it out to be on television. There are many more costs and considerations than what they show on TV. Flipping is not always a glamorous business where you make $100,000 on a single deal. To me, flipping is more about earning consistent, smaller profits on multiple houses at once. This reduces risks and keeps you on your toes! I have made over $100,000 on three different flips, but those were very unique situations.

I like to flip in the lower price ranges where I do not have as many costs and cash committed to a deal. My average purchase price in 2017 has been around $140,000, and my average selling price is close to $220,000. I average about $35,000 in repairs on each flip. I happen to be in Colorado, which has one of the hottest markets in the country. In fact, my county was just named one of the top 4 most unaffordable counties in the nation. Why do I mention this? Many people will say the time to flip houses has passed and you cannot flip in a hot seller's market. However, I am flipping more houses now than I ever have, without sacrificing my profit margins or depending on price increases. This book goes through everything I do and leaves nothing out. If you want to start fixing and flipping or want to improve your fix and flip business, you found the right book!

Part 1: Money

1. How Much Money Can You Make Fixing and Flipping Houses?

Many television shows make fixing and flipping houses look glamorous. They show how easy it is to buy a house at an auction, how quickly you can repair a house, and how people can make huge amounts. The truth is, there is a lot more work involved in flipping houses than what you see on TV. Most of the costs are not listed on television, and it takes much longer to flip a house than the time they portray in shows. It takes a lot of money, a lot of work, and a lot time to make money from house flipping. It also takes a lot of math. A key element to flipping is calculating costs and profits before you ever buy a property, and many beginners do not take the time to properly determine the costs involved in a flip.

We will discuss specific costs in later chapters, but for now, let us look at what I make on my flips and what you could realistically earn in most markets.

Once you develop a system, you can make a lot of money. I am by no means at the top of the flipper totem pole. Many investors fix and flip many more houses than I do. Flipping can provide great income, but flipping is not a weekend project. You need to have a business and systems in place to be able to flip multiple houses at once.

How much money can you make on a single fix and flip?

The money you make on a flip varies with each deal and hinges on the value of the house. I have lost $10,000 and made up to $100,000. My goal on each fix and flip is to make at least $25,000. I have hit some home runs and have had some huge mishaps. There is a lot of risk involved in the process, and if I do not have at least $25,000 in profit potential, I usually will not make the deal. The more expensive a house is, the more money I need to make because there is more risk in more expensive houses.

My average profit is about $33,000 after taking into account all the costs that go into a flip, including carrying costs, financing costs, buying costs, repairs, and selling costs.

The more expensive a fix and flip, the more money you should make

Pricier houses should net you more money than less expensive ones. The more expensive a house, the more repairs, interest, holding costs, and commissions you pay. Because of the increased risk inherent in higher-value houses, you need to be rewarded with increased profit.

It also takes more capital to buy and repair a more expensive house. If I have a profit potential of $25,000 on a $100,000 fix and flip, I want a profit potential of $50,000 on a $200,000 one. And, when I buy a more expensive house, I will not be able to buy as many properties since I am using more cash for down payments and repairs.

How much money have I made flipping houses?

I sold 17 fix and flips in 2016, and the total profits were well over $450,000. It was not easy to flip that many houses, and I plan to flip twice as many in 2017! Because our market is hot, I have not lowered my profit potential but instead have expanded the way I find deals in order to flip that many houses. I have also been growing the business bigger and bigger by reinvesting most of my profits.

I did not start out flipping this many houses. My father and I partnered on many deals and may have flipped four houses per year if we were lucky. He had been flipping long before I started and had a ton of experience. While it is possible to make a lot of money, do not expect to make hundreds of thousands of dollars your first year. There are many roadblocks for beginners, including getting the money together, finding contractors, finding deals, and learning your market.

You have to fix and flip a lot of houses to make money

I would love to make $100,000 on each fix and flip, but that is not always possible in my market. I am in Northern Colorado, where the average house price is $260,000. I buy most of my flips for less than $150,000. If you are in an area with a $750,000 average price, it may be easier to make $100,000 on a flip. In fact, at that price, because of the risks involved, I would want any flip of mine to make $100,000. For the most part, I will talk about lower-priced flips because the average price in the United States is very close to the average price in my market. We will discuss some flips that are more expensive as well.

I don't always know which houses will succeed as flips and which won't. Sometimes, unforeseen circumstances have caused me to hold a property for a year before it sold. That killed my profits and was one of the houses on which I lost money. I have accepted that some flips will be great and others will not. If I continue to find great deals, the averages will be in my favor. My strategy is to buy as many fix and flips that meet my criteria as possible and continue to average $30,000 in profit on each property. Some will make less and some will make more. Even after many years in the business, I cannot always predict which houses will do the best.

If you are only flipping one house, I hope you start out with a good one. However, there is a chance you could lose money no matter how great the deal looks in the beginning. The trick is to keep flipping. If you know what you are doing and keep working hard, you will make money. I interview many awesome flippers on my podcast, and many of them lost money on their first flip. They did not give up; they kept working and learned how to make money from both their good and bad experiences.

How to avoid losing money on a fix and flip

Here are a few quick tips on how to avoid losing money. We will go into more detail in later chapters.

- Be very cautious at foreclosure auctions. I used to buy 90 percent of my deals at foreclosure auctions. You are required to pay cash, without a title policy, and sometimes you are not able to see the interior of the house. If you buy at a foreclosure sale, make sure you have a lot of leeway for repairs, title issues, and possible evictions.
- Always plan more for repairs than you estimate. Repairs always cost more, and more repairs always show up when fixing a house. I always assume repair costs will exceed my estimates by 20 percent.
- Account for financing and selling costs. You must pay a real estate commission, title insurance, homeowners insurance, taxes, utilities, interest on financing, and more when you flip a property.
- Be conservative when you estimate value, and price the house right! Fix and flippers realize some of their biggest losses from overpriced houses, and often, they don't lower the price quickly enough to get them sold.

Conclusion

Fixing and flipping is not easy. It takes patience when searching for properties, money to fix them up, and market knowledge to sell them. If you can master fix and flips, you can earn awesome income. You can also have a lot of fun. Becoming a successful fix and flipper does not happen overnight. The rest of the book will discuss many tips and tricks I use to make money through flipping and will teach the basics that many people tend to ignore. Fundamentals make the money, and if you ignore the basics, you get in trouble.

2. How Much Money Do You Need to Fix and Flip a House?

You usually must spend money to make money. You may hear stories of investors fixing and flipping houses without using any of their own money, but these investors are usually very experienced flippers or they are giving up most of their profits. Hard-money lenders can allow investors to complete a fix and flip with less money, but hard-money lenders are very expensive. Using either a partner or private money can also reduce the amount of money an investor needs. However, unless you are very well established, you may have to give up a percentage of your profits to use these techniques.

How much money does an investor need to fix and flip using hard money?

There are many hard-money lenders, and they each set different terms and conditions on their loans. Some hard-money lenders claim they will allow an investor to buy, renovate, and sell a fix and flip without any of their own money. However, most hard-money lenders will only give these terms to an experienced fix and flipper with a proven record of success. If the investor is just getting started, the lender will require either money up front or a share of the profits. The hard-money lender will also want to ensure the fix and flip will be profitable and will keep a very close eye on the project.

If you are using a hard-money lender, count on needing some money for down payments and repairs. Some hard-money lenders may require more or less than others, depending on the deal and the investor's experience. You may be able to get the hard-money lender to fund most of the deal if you share 50 percent of the profits. Either way, this type of lender is not cheap: 2 to 5 points and 10 to 15 percent (you may be able to find hard-money rates at 8 percent now) interest is common.

How much money will you need to fix and flip with a partner?

I know many fix and flippers who use partners to help fund deals. I used to work with my father on our fix and flips; he would fund the deals, and I would do most of the work. I see many flippers who find deals, repair the house, and sell them, but still need a partner to help pay for the fix and flip. A 50/50 split is very common in these deals. Usually, one partner puts up the money and the other does all the work. This may seem like an unfair split considering one person is doing all the work, but without the money, you cannot do the deal.

This is one way to get started, but giving up 50 percent of your profit is a big deal. I think any flipper should set a goal where they save enough of their own money to start paying for down payments and repairs. When you give up 50 percent of your profit, it is hard to save enough money to start funding your own deals.

With a partner, it is possible to complete a fix and flip without any of your own money, but you will make much less. Instead of making $30,000 on a house, you may only make $17,000 (no financing costs with a partner).

How much money will you need to fix and flip with bank financing?

It is not easy, but it is possible, to fix and flip using bank financing. I use a portfolio lender to fund my fix and flips, and they are awesome. They give me 80 percent of the purchase price and charge me one point on my short-term fix and flip financing. Instead of the 15 percent a hard-money lender would charge, my lender charges 5.25 percent.

My lender does not fund any of the repairs, but some portfolio lenders will. Every portfolio lender has different terms and guidelines for how much money they will lend and at what rates. I am required to put down 20 percent of the purchase price and pay for repairs on each house. That can add up to anywhere from $45,000 to $60,000 on a $100,000 purchase, depending on how many repairs are needed. That seems like a lot of money, but by using my own money, I save thousands on the both the interest rate and points a hard-money lender would charge. And since I don't use a partner, I also get to keep all the profits. Finally, I do not use all of my own money to pay for these expenses since I also use private money.

How much money do you need to fix and flip with private money?

Private money is an investor's best friend if you can find the right person offering the right terms. Most private money comes from someone you know: a family member, a friend, or a business acquaintance. Many people are looking for a low-risk way to invest and earn great returns. Investing in a fix and flip business can help you achieve high returns without much risk, depending on the situation. A brand new fix-and-flipper is more risky in the lender's eyes than an investor who has completed 50 fix and flips. You can use real estate as collateral for private money to give the lender more assurance you will pay it back.

Because there are different levels of risk involved with every deal and each lender expects a different level of return, private-money terms vary greatly. Because I am a very seasoned investor, I pay as little as 6-10 percent interest, and I offer my lender great collateral. Other private lenders may expect 10 percent or even 15 percent interest on their money based on the risk. The hardest part about getting private money is finding someone to lend it to you. You cannot be afraid to ask around to see if anyone you know would be interested in lending you money and earning higher returns in the process.

With private money, it is possible to get started with no out-of-pocket money. It may be hard to find a lender that will fund your entire deal, but it is the best way to get started using as little of your own money as possible while still keeping your profits.

Conclusion

In order to fix and flip a house, you are typically going to have to use some of your own money or split a large chunk of the profits with a partner. To make the most money, a combination of bank financing, private money, and your own money is the best route. It is hard work saving enough to get started, but it is well worth it in the end. Buying a house, fixing it up, and selling it, requires a lot of time and risk. I want to earn as much money as possible for taking on that risk. If you want to flip houses and do not have a private money lender, expect to pay cash for at least 20 percent of the total project to make the deal work.

3. What Are the Costs Involved in Flipping?

If you are not aware of the costs involved, you can lose a lot of money. There are basic costs like down payments and repairs, but investors overlook many other costs. You must account for financing costs, closing costs, carrying costs, repair costs, and selling costs. You must also account for the time and effort you put into the process. If you are doing all the repairs yourself, you must decide what your time is worth.

What financing costs are involved with flipping houses?

I love to buy long-term rentals because they provide cash flow month after month. Long-term rentals are also easier to finance than fix and flips. Banks do not like to loan on fix and flips because they can only charge interest for the short time that you own the house. If you can find a bank to finance a fix and flip, they will most likely charge a higher interest rate and charge more upfront costs than they would on a long-term loan. I have a great relationship with my portfolio lender. They charge 5.25 percent interest and a one percent origination fee with 80 percent loan-to-value ratios. It will be very difficult for a beginning investor to find these terms without a proven record.

Hard-money lenders are another option for fix and flippers, but as I previously mentioned, they will charge much more than my bank. A hard-money lender will charge a higher interest rate (10 to 15 percent), and higher origination fees (two to four percent). However, a hard-money lender may finance more than 75 percent of the purchase price along with some of the repairs.

If you would like a list of nationwide hard-money lenders, shoot me an email at Mark@investFourMore.com.

Here are the minimum and maximum financing costs on a fix and flip held for six months:

$75,000 bank loan (my terms)

Origination charge:	$1,125
Interest over six months:	$1,969
Total:	**$3,093**

$90,000 hard-money loan

Origination:	$3,600
Interest over six months:	$6,750
Total:	**$10,350**

What are the buying costs of a fix and flip?

There are more costs than just those involved in financing. Some sellers, like HUD, do not pay the buyer's title insurance or closing fees. There are recording fees and closing fees, and in some cases, you may have to pay the insurance and taxes. Some banks may require an appraisal, flood certification, and other fees as well.

Most buyers will want some type of inspection before deciding to purchase a house. An inspection can cost $200 to $600 depending on the location and size of the house. With a HUD home, the buyer will have to pay for the inspection and for utilities to be turned on.

Estimated buying costs on a fix and flip: **$500 to $2,500**

What are the carrying costs on a fix and flip?

When you buy a fix and flip, there will be many carrying costs for the time you own the house. You will need to pay insurance, taxes, utilities, HOA dues, and yard maintenance until you sell the house.

Estimated carrying costs on a $100,000 house for six months:

Insurance:	$700
Taxes:	$500-2500
Utilities:	$1,500
HOA:	$0-$2,500
Yard maintenance:	$600
Total:	**$3,300-7,800**

What does it cost to sell a fix and flip?

Selling a house is not cheap. You must pay real estate agents and many other costs at closing. Each state charges different costs to sell a house, so before you buy a fix and flip, be sure to confirm what it costs to sell a house in your state.

Here are the estimated costs of selling a $150,000 house in Colorado (all commissions are negotiable):

Real estate commissions:	$9,000
Title insurance:	$900
Recording fees:	$200
Closing fee:	$200
Buyers closing costs:	$4,500
Total selling costs:	**$14,800**

What are the total costs required to fix and flip a house?

The total costs that go into a fix and flip may surprise you. You need approximately $17,000 to $30,850 just to take care of the financing, carrying costs, buying costs, and selling costs. This does not include the repair costs and out-of-pocket cash that you will need to complete the flip. Once you figure in the repairs, you are going to spend at least $30,000 on a house you buy for $100,000. The more expensive the house, the higher the costs. I made almost $50,000 on the last fix and flip I did, but I had a $100,000 margin between the buying and selling price on that house.

4. How Long Does It Take to Fix and Flip a House?

My biggest challenge when fixing and flipping is repairing and selling houses quickly. On the surface, you would think that you could flip a house in three months. You simply buy the property, fix it, list it, and sell it. However, it usually takes me at least twice that long. It takes time to find and schedule contractors, complete repairs, ensure the repairs were done correctly, and sell the house. One of my goals is to reduce the time it takes me to flip so I can buy more properties and make more money.

What is the most difficult and time-consuming part of fixing and flipping?

As I mentioned, finding quality, timely contractors is one of my biggest challenges. I use a mix of contractors and subcontractors to repair my houses. Because they are specialists and are really good at what they do, I try to use as many subs as I can. The subcontractors can usually finish their work while I am waiting for the main contractor to finish another house. The tough part is managing the contractors and subs when doing 15 or 20 flips at once. Luckily, I have an awesome team, and Nikki, my project manager, is amazing. She makes sure everyone is doing what they are supposed to. There is no way I could do it all on my own.

Why does it take so long to repair a fix and flip?

If I had only one or two flips going at one time, I could greatly reduce the time it takes to repair a house. However, I must wait for my contractors to finish one job before they can start another. No matter how often my contractors say they can handle multiple jobs at once, they always have problems when I give them more than one job at a time. I usually spend $25,000 to $35,000 in repairs on my fix and flips, and it usually takes my contractors 8 to 12 weeks to complete the job. The reason it takes so long for them to complete a job is there are many tasks involved in getting a house repaired.

- I have to meet with the contractor and decide what to repair.
- I must wait for the contractor to put a bid together (always get a bid!).
- I must decide if the bid is reasonable and if we need to make any changes.
- Once I approve the job, I must wait for the contractor to clear his schedule to get the job done.
- Once the contractor starts the job, something unexpected always comes up that extends the timeline.
- Once the contractor finished, I have to make sure nothing needs to be corrected or we did not forget anything.
- Once the job is complete, we must get the house cleaned and ready to list.

I wish I could count on four-week turnaround times, but it does not happen. Contractors always come up with reasons why they had delays and could not finish on time. I am currently working on hiring my own employees to work on properties so that I have complete control of the process.

How long does it take to list a fix and flip after you repair it?

Once a house is repaired and ready to list, the fun begins. I am a real estate agent, so listing the house is relatively easy for me. I do not have to wait for another agent to list the house, nor do I spend time finding a real estate agent. It also takes time to choose the listing price. You do not want to list too high, or you will scare away buyers. List the house too low and you are leaving money on the table. This is why it is so important to use a real estate agent. I can list my fix and flips listed within a couple of days. Then, I wait for an offer to come in. For non-agent investors, it can take much longer to list a house.

How long does it take to sell a fix and flip after you list it?

Once you list a house, you have to wait for an offer, negotiate the offer, and wait for the closing process. The closing process includes buyer inspections, an appraisal, and loan approvals. In my experience, if I list a house for the right price, I usually receive a good offer in about three weeks. Once a contract is in place, it can take from four to six weeks to close on the house. Ideally, there are no problems with appraisals, inspections, or the buyer's loan, but if there are, the process repeats.

Our market is really crazy right now and has record low inventory. It does not surprise us to see multiple offers on a house the first few days it is listed, even when priced right. The three-week time period for an offer is normal in a market with equal supply and demand.

What is the total time it takes to complete a fix and flip?

If you add up all the time it takes to complete a flip, you may be surprised how long it takes. If it takes me 10 weeks to make repairs, one week to list the house, and eight weeks to sell it, I come up with 19 weeks to complete the flip. That's in a perfect world. This timeframe assumes I met the contractors immediately after I bought the house, priced the house right, and there were no delays when I tried to sell it. Unfortunately, contracts sometimes fall through, which can add another eight weeks to the process. If a buyer is using hard money to finance a fix and flip, you must account for delays that could add thousands of dollars to the cost of. I count on every flip taking six months from purchase to sale.

How can you save time on a fix and flip?

Here are some tips to help you save time when flipping:

- Meet with your contractors at the house before you close. Have them scheduled to start as soon as the house is yours.
- Meet with your real estate agent before the repairs are complete so you have a price and are ready to list.
- Price the house right to begin with and do not get greedy!
- Lower the price if you do not get an acceptable offer in the first month.
- Stay in constant contact with your contractor and make sure they know the deadlines (they easily forget them).

Conclusion

The time it takes to complete a flip catches many people off guard, and you must account for it in the holding costs. There are ways to decrease the time it takes to flip a house, but many unforeseeable things can greatly increase that time. Do your best to flip a house quickly, but be prepared to hold on to the property for longer than you thought.

5. How I Made $35,000 on a Flip without Making Repairs

I have spent a lot of time improving my flipping business over the last year. I have some bad experiences thanks to a project manager I hired who did not work out. I've also had some really good experiences. Recently, I had a great experience when I earned $35,000 on a flip...without making any repairs. I bought the house from the MLS, and a tenant was already living there. Despite my best attempts to avoid eviction, the tenant was evicted. I sold the house for about $47,000 more than I bought it for. I know some investors might say they made $47,000 in this situation, but I try to be realistic with the costs that come with flipping houses, even when I don't make repairs.

How was I able to get such a great deal from the MLS?

I bought this property for $102,344 on March 18th, 2016. The house was listed for $75,000 and was an estate sale. The property next door was also part of the estate sale, and I bought that one as well for about $118,000. We repaired the house next door, which we sold for close to $200,000. At $75,000, this house was listed well below market value. It is really hard to find any decent houses for less than $150,000, so I knew I wanted to buy this house. The house was listed on the MLS, and I went to see both houses as soon as I possibly could. Since I am a real estate agent, I made an appointment to see the house next door, which was vacant, but I could not set up an appointment right away because it was occupied.

While I was at the house next door, the tenants were out in the yard of the $75,000 house. I knew it might take at least a day, via an appointment, to see the house, so I talked to the tenants. They were nice and offered to let me see the inside. The house

29

was a two-unit property with one unit upstairs and one unit in the basement. I was only able to view the upstairs unit, and it needed some work but was not in horrible condition. At $75,000, I knew this was an amazing deal since the house would be worth at least $180,000 after repairs. I made full-price offers on both houses the first day they were listed, with a quick close date and no inspection contingencies.

I was hoping that, since I made the offers about three hours after the houses were listed, the seller would quickly accept the offers, but they received multiple offers the first day. I had to decide how much I wanted to offer to give myself room for profit and have a chance to buy them. I like to offer weird numbers, especially in a highest-and-best situation. I offered $102,344 (for the houses that was listed for $75,000) because it made the seller think I put more thought into the offer, and if someone offers $102,000, mine will be slightly higher. Even though the house was listed for $75,000, I had no problem offering much more because I knew I could still make a good profit. A couple of days later, the listing agent told me both of my offers had been accepted, even though they had over 20 offers on each house.

Why was this house listed so cheap?

When a house is occupied, it can be much harder to sell it. Owner-occupied buyers will purchase most houses, and they cannot move in while the house is under lease. This particular house also needed some work that would not allow a buyer to get an FHA or conventional loan. The same lady had rented it for many years, and she only paid $375 per month, even though average rents were $1,000 per month. She was on a month-to-month lease, and the seller had asked whoever bought the house not to kick her out right away. The basement unit was rented for about $500 per month, which was closer to market averages but still a little low. If you considered the current rent on the property, the condition, and that fact it was tenant occupied, I could see why the house was listed a little lower than market value. However, I think $75,000 was far too low, even for this house.

How was I able to get the tenants out?

Both tenants were on a month-to-month lease, which meant that I could end the lease with 30 days' notice. I promised not to kick the tenant out right away, but I was not told how long "right away" meant. I could have ended the leases and gotten away with it, but I don't operate that way, and I had many other flips going at the same time. The tenant wanted to stay as long as possible and keep paying the $375 per month. We asked when she might want to move and even offered money to make it easier for her to move out. The problem was she could not afford much more than she was paying, and there are very few rentals in the area with rent under $700 per month that include the most basic amenities. We agreed to let her stay another three months to give her time to find another place, and we agreed not to raise her existing rent.

As the move-out date neared, she stopped answering her phone. We could not reach her but could tell she was still living there. We left notes, messages, and letters saying we needed to talk to her and would even pay her to move out by the agreed upon date. She still would not respond, so we decided to start the eviction process. It is very easy to evict someone in Colorado if they break their lease. It takes about 4 weeks to complete the entire process. When we started the eviction process, she finally contacted us and begged us not to evict her because she could not find a new place. I could tell she was never going to move on her own and we would have to continue with the eviction process. If she didn't leave by the eviction deadline, we would have to hire a crew to move all her stuff onto the street. Luckily, she moved out right before the deadline, and we took possession of the house. The tenant in the other house was much easier to work with and was happy to take our money to find a new place to rent.

Why did I choose to sell this house as-is?

I repair almost every flip I buy, but I decided to try to sell this home as-is. I knew I got a great deal on it, and most of the work involved evacuating the tenants. Once the tenants were gone, I decided to list the house on the MLS. I listed it for $159,000, which made it one of the cheapest houses on the market. I was hoping to get an investor-buyer who would use the property as a rental.

I received a couple of offers right away, but they were from owner-occupied buyers who would need a loan. I talked to the buyer's agents and told them the house would not qualify for a loan due to some issues, including a roof that needed work. One agent insisted his buyer wanted the house and the bank would loan on the house in its current condition, except for the roof. I agreed to raise the price above the listing price and replace the roof. Because additional work may have been needed after the inspection, we decided not to replace the roof until after the inspection and appraisal deadlines passed. The buyers completed their inspection and asked us to do much more work on the house, even though we told them the roof was all we would do and the house was priced very fairly. We could not agree on a resolution, so I put the house back on the market. I should have known better than to try to sell the house to owner occupants in its current condition.

Within two weeks of relisting the house, a cash investor bought it for $149,000.

How much money did I make on this house?

I bought this house using a portfolio-lender loan. I financed 75 percent of the purchase price for one point and a 4.5 percent interest rate (I have a couple of different lenders I work with and recently found a lender with even lower rates). Below are all the costs on the deal:

Purchase price:	$102,344
Taxes and insurance:	$1,500
Utilities, maintenance:	$500
Eviction/trash-out:	$2,000
Financing costs:	$3,000
Selling costs:	$5,000
Total:	**$114,344**

Since I sold the house for $149,000, I made just under $35,000. I may have been able to make a little more had I fixed it up, but that would have taken me at least two more months. I was working 11 flips at the time, and I cannot repair many of my houses right away because my contractors are working on other jobs. I was happy to take a quick profit.

Conclusion

I make repairs on most of the houses I buy, but I have flipped a few houses this year where I did not make any repairs. Last year, I bought a house for $105,000 that was occupied by the previous owners. I rented it back to them for about a year for $1,300 per month and sold it for $145,000. I sold a flip last year for $20,000 more than my purchase price without making repairs and without another agent. Also, I currently have a flip in my inventory that I may sell to certain investors without doing a full rehab. It is fun to see the transformation on a house after we fix it up, but it is also nice to make a quick profit.

6. How to Make One Million Dollars within a Year by Flipping Houses

I have never made one million dollars within a year by flipping houses, but it is fun to contemplate. It is possible, but it takes a lot of work and planning. Fixing and flipping has been a great additional income source for me, but as you have seen, it takes patience, hard work, and time to build up your business.

How many flips would I have to complete to make one million dollars within a year?

At my current profit margin, I would have to flip just over 30 houses. That is a lot of flips, but many investors flip that many or more every year. I heard an investor speak at a conference who flipped over 1,200 houses in one year! I flipped 17 houses in 2016, which is not too far away from 30. I actually have a goal to flip 30 houses in 2017, but it will take a lot of hard work and new systems to reach that goal.

How much money would I have to invest to make one million dollars?

I need at least $45,000 in cash on each flip. However, many times I need more. If a house needs more repairs or is more expensive, I need more cash. In some instances, I need less. Despite my $45,000 figure, I always assume I'll need a bit more, so I assume $55,000 for each flip. I have some private money and a paid-off line of credit on my rental property. That totals $280,000. For 10 flips at $55,000 each, I need $550,000. That means I use $270,000 of my own money if I'm working 10 flips. If I had 30 flips, I would need a lot more cash because I would have to flip at least 15 houses at once. I am actually doing that now, but it is taking a ton of cash.

How many fix-and-flips would I need at one time to make one million dollars within a year?

I am averaging over six months, from purchase to sale, per flip. However, I know I could flip houses faster with more contractors and better systems. I assume I will be able to complete all upcoming fix-and-flips in six months or less. That means I would always need to have 15 flips going at once to reach 30 houses per year.

If I have 15 houses going at any one time, I'd need $775,000 ($55,000 per property). After deducting my line of credit and private money, I would still need $495,000 in cash. If I wanted to expand my operation, I could find more private money or get a partner. However, I don't want a partner because I would have to share my profits. In the last year, I have found more private-money lenders who will lend me 100 percent of the purchase price on my purchases. The rates are higher (10 to 12 percent), but I'm into the deal for much less cash. I have also found a hard-money lender that will give me 85 percent of the purchase price and 100 percent of the repairs at an 8.75 percent interest rate and 2.75 percent points.

How hard would it be to finance 15 flips at once?

My portfolio lender has a great program for my flipping business. However, they limit my total borrowing ability to $750,000, and I am very close to that limit. If I had 15 flips going at once, I would need to borrow at least $1,000,000. If I wanted to flip 30 houses per year, I would have to amend the deal with my bank and hope they would go for it.

In the last year, my bank raised my limit to one million dollars, and I also found another local lender who would lend me money for my flips.

Could my contractors handle 15 flips at once?

Another issue I would have with completing 30 flips per year and 15 at one time is finding enough contractors. I have five contractors who are doing a great job for me now. However, I am not their only customer, and it takes at least 60 days to finish the repairs on most of my flips. Usually, it takes longer than 60 days, even though the contractor never seems to think it will when they start the job!

If I kept my current contractors and they only worked on my properties, they could complete five flips in one month, five the next month, and the final five the next month. That assumes I buy all fifteen flips at once. For me to flip 30 houses in a year, I only need to buy 2.5 flips every month. That means I could get by with five contractors if I spread out my purchases. Technically, if all five contractors worked for me and completed one flip per month, they could complete 60 in one year. I still have my plan to buy 100 rental properties, and I will need contractors to work on those properties as well. If I planned everything perfectly, I could probably get it all done, but that rarely happens, so I would need to find even more contractors!

Could I find enough deals to make one million dollars within a year?

The biggest challenge when flipping houses is finding great deals. I have always been able to find deals in the past, whether through auctions, the MLS, or direct marketing. However, I have not bought 2.5 deals every month. My 2017 goal has been to buy 3 deals per month, and I have come really close.

I have been expanding the ways I buy houses. I think there is still opportunity to buy at foreclosure sales, even though I have not attended one for months. If the number of foreclosures on the market starts to grow or a couple of foreclosure investors stop buying or move away, there may be more opportunity. I bought one house at a foreclosure sale recently. I also found another source: wholesalers, who have been feeding me deals like crazy lately. In fact, in 2017, I've averaged 2 wholesale purchase deals per month.

What if I increased my profit by buying more expensive flips?

Another option to hit the one-million-per-year figure is to look for more expensive properties. There is a lot of risk involved with buying more expensive flips, and I would expect much more profit per deal. A pricier flip requires a larger down payment, more interest charges, more carrying costs and—usually—more repairs. The more expensive a house, the nicer it should be, and the more expensive the remodel. Higher-priced flips also take longer to sell because there are fewer prospective buyers in higher price ranges.

If I buy pricier flips, I want my profit percentage to be similar to my lower-priced flips. If I make $30,000 on an $80,000 flip, I would expect to make $60,000 on a $160,000 flip. The problem with those profit margins is they are hard to find. Flippers in my area are content to make $25,000 to $30,000 on a flip that costs them $160,000 or even $200,000.

In my experience, I usually do not make enough on a higher-price flip to justify the extra costs and risks involved. I have made over $100,000 on only two flips in the last 13 years, but deals like those are not readily available and, in my opinion, were flukes. Over the years, I have learned that lower-end properties make more money in my market. Therefore, I choose not to pursue higher-priced properties.

I did perform one high-end flip recently. It was a unique situation where the tenant was still occupying the property and did not want to leave. I bought the property for $535,000, and 14 months later, I sold it for $802,000. I only spent $35,000 on repairs and made a nice profit, but I don't expect to see those results again anytime soon. For details on the property, search for high-end flip and InvestFourMore on Google.

What would I have to do to make one million dollars within a year?

After analyzing my situation and what it would take to hit one million dollars, I realized it is possible. It would take a lot of work and some adjustments to my business model. Here is a breakdown of what I would have to do:

1. **Save more money for fixing and flipping or find more private money**. If I were to save all profits from my current flips, I would have nearly enough after taxes.
2. **Reduce my turn time to six months or less**. If I lower my turn time for ten simultaneous flips, I could flip 20 houses per year, which would greatly increase my income, but still leave me short of one million. Now that I have five great contractors, I can reduce my turn time to six months, but I might need another great contractor to reach 30 flips per year.
3. **Ask for more money from my lender to finance 15 flips at once**. My lender may or may not do this; I have not yet asked them about increasing my limit. I have already figured this one out with my lender and by adding a new lender!

4. **Expand my flipping area and look non-stop all year for deals**. I think it is possible to find 30 flips per year, but it would be tough. It also might take time away from my rental properties or real estate business, causing them to suffer. If I could make one million per year through flipping, it would be worth it.

Conclusion

I think it is possible for me to make one million dollars by flipping 30 houses per year. Whether I want to or not, I have not decided to pursue this because I still want to have plenty of time for my family. Also, my real estate team is doing great, my rental properties are very lucrative, and I love writing for *InvestFourMore.com*. I am not sure I could continue doing everything I am doing now and flip 30 houses per year. I do want to continue to grow my flipping business and move more houses each year. Who knows? Maybe eventually I will get to 30 flips per year and reach that million-dollar mark.

I first wrote this chapter in 2014, when I was nowhere close to flipping 30 houses within a year. In 2017, I am close and may actually reach my million-dollar goal. I have improved my financing, deal sourcing, and management. It is really cool to see the process and what setting goals can do.

Part 2: What are the Risks and Rewards of Flipping Houses?

7. Why I Like to Fix and Flip Houses: Money, Time, Enjoyment...

I run a retail real estate team, and I flip houses. I also run *InvestFourMore.com* and own rental properties. It is not easy to run any of these businesses, but I can say that fixing and flipping provides the most profit by far for the time invested. I can find flips in almost any market at any time. I am an REO agent, and I have little control over how many REOs I list. It all depends on the market. My rental properties make me money, but those are a long-term play. My blog is a ton of fun and I love doing it, but it takes a lot of time.

I can make $30,000 on a flip, and I complete 20 to 30 per year. I've set up my flipping business to run without needing my constant oversight. However, I love finding deals, and flipping houses is very fun and rewarding.

Why does it take less time to fix and flip than it does to sell houses as a real estate agent?

It has taken me many years to build up a team that can help me with all my real estate activities. They help with all facets of listing houses, working with buyers, completing tasks on my REOs, and helping with the fix and flips. It takes a lot of time to work with buyers and sell a house. It also takes a lot of time to list houses for regular sellers or banks, although you can make a lot of money selling real estate as a real estate agent.

Flipping houses takes time, but much of that time involves managing contractors during the repair process. If you can get great contractors who can handle the repair process without a lot of oversight, it takes minimal time to manage a flip. I spend most of my time finding properties at below market value and reviewing potential deals. It takes some time to list and sell a house, but not as much time as it takes to list an REO or someone else's house. I do not have to contact anyone else or complete any tasks because it is my house, and I get to make all the decisions.

I have a lot of fun fixing and flipping houses

One of the things I love about fixing and flipping houses is it is fun. It is cool to turn a crappy old house into a nicely updated house that a family would be proud to live in. There are ups and downs, and there are always unexpected costs, but it is all worth it. I have come to expect at least one major unexpected cost on each fix and flip, so I always budget about 20 percent more for unknown costs. I am at the point where I have 10 to 20 flips going at one time, and I know some of the properties will do great and others will have issues. Overall, good fix and flips will make up for the bad ones.

It is also fun receiving one big check from the sale. I put 25 percent down when I flip; plus, I make repairs, and then I sell a house for much more than I bought it for. At closings, I routinely receive checks that range from $60,000 to $100,000. That is not all profit, but it sure feels good to hold checks that big!

Buying houses is a rush. I know that, when I get a great deal on a house, I will most likely profit. Getting a great deal also means I out-maneuvered, acted faster than, or did something else better than the heavy competition in my area. Buying houses is almost as much fun as selling them! Some say I am addicted to buying houses, and I cannot disagree with them.

Fixing and flipping has allowed me to buy more rental properties

It takes a great deal of cash to fix and flip houses. Even with a hard-money lender, you will need some of your own cash to make a deal work well. You need a lot of money to flip multiple houses, and I have saved much of the money I make and put it right back into the flipping business.

I have also used my profits to buy more rental properties. Even though flipping brings in a lot of money in the short-term, rental properties will keep producing income as long as I own them. Rental properties are also expensive, and my flipping income has allowed me to buy many more rentals than I otherwise could have.

Fixing and flipping is less stressful than most real estate jobs

This may not be true for everyone, especially if you are working on your flip, but flipping can be less stressful than selling a house for someone else. I love fixing and flipping because I have control over the entire process. Since I am the owner of the house, I get to make the decisions regarding cost, repairs, tricky situations that may come up, and the sale.

When I am listing houses either for banks or for other people, I must always answer to a seller. I must run every situation by that seller and help them make the best decisions. That is not always easy to do, especially with some banks. Many traditional sellers rely on their emotions more than they do facts. As an agent, that can be tricky, especially if you are dealing with friends or family. Because I have complete control over the fix-and-flip process, I find it is much less stressful than selling houses for other people.

Conclusion

I love fixing and flipping and will continue to do it for the near future. I love that it does not take all my time; I love the money it produces; and I love the process itself. I also love the other parts of my real estate business. I think it is very important to have multiple streams of income. Right now, my REO listings are way down because there is so little REO in our area, but my fix and flips have done great.

8. What Are the Possible Downfalls Involved in Flipping Houses?

Not everything is peachy in house flipping. At times, I have been stressed out and have lost money. If you do your job right and account for all circumstances, you should be able to limit your losses. The most I have ever lost on a flip was about $10,000. The most I have made is about $100,000. I think the positives still outweigh the negatives, but you need to know what you are getting into.

Flips take time and may not be as easy as you think

I am in a position where my team helps with many of the flipping activities. It took me a long time to get to this point, and most beginners will not have the help that I have. If you think you can buy a house, work on it yourself on the weekends, sell it in a month or two, and make a huge profit, you are probably fooling yourself. There is a lot involved, and if you try to do all the work yourself on top of your other responsibilities, you are asking for trouble.

If you want to do the work yourself, make sure to calculate how much time the work will take. Then plan how many hours you are going to work each week. Remember, you will probably work less than you plan for, and the work will take longer than you think. I have seen investors try to complete the work themselves in one month and then find it takes six months and the experience is so horrible they swear off real estate investing for good. I made this mistake a few years ago, and there is an entire chapter devoted to this subject later.

It is hard to find good deals!

There are many real estate investors in most markets. That means there is a lot of competition. If you think you can hop on Zillow and find three houses that can be flipped, think again. At times, it takes me months of scouring the market to find good deals. I am a full-time real estate agent, and I have a huge advantage over those who have another job or are flipping on the side.

It will take a lot of work and time to find great deals. You will need to find an awesome real estate agent if you are not one yourself, and you will have to be able to find deals yourself as well.

It is difficult to find great contractors

The key to my flipping success is finding great deals and great contractors. A bad contractor can cost you tens of thousands of dollars. Before you ever flip a house, make sure you have a trustworthy contractor.

The market can change

Many flippers went bankrupt during the last housing crisis because they had multiple flips going and the market dropped like a rock. They could not sell their houses fast enough, and they lost them to foreclosure. You must be on top of your market and sell your flips quickly to avoid possible market changes.

There are many costs involved

There are many more costs than just those for repairs. Many investors make the mistake of miscalculating costs and end up losing money. You must know what all the costs will be before you buy a house; you cannot just assume there is enough room to cover everything.

Repairs always cost more than you think

When flipping, repairs always cost more than the estimate. This does not happen because the contractor is trying to screw you but because you cannot know everything that's wrong with a house until the repairs have begun. Once demolition begins, you begin see problems that you could not see before you bought the house. I always assume there will be more repairs than estimated. In addition, it usually takes longer to make repairs. I always assume it will take me longer to complete a flip than I estimate.

Conclusion

There is a lot of risk in flipping, but if do your homework and plan for the unexpected, you should be ready for the curveballs that come your way. Always plan for the flip to take longer and to cost more than you think it will.

9. Why It Is Risky to Buy Old Houses to Flip

One of the biggest risks in house flipping houses is buying old houses. I flip old houses, but you must know what you are doing. The older a house, the more likely it's going to have serious problems and need major repairs.

I invest in many fix and flips and rentals every year, and I would love it if they were all ten years old or newer. The newer a house, the fewer repairs it needs and the quicker you can complete the repairs. In reality, we cannot always choose the perfect rental or fix-and-flip house. I like to buy properties at below market value, and I do not always have the option of buying a newer house that's in great shape. If I do buy an older house, I carefully review the necessary repairs, and I make sure I am getting a great deal.

There is a lot of competition in real estate, and sometimes I buy questionable houses. I flipped a house in 2014 that was built in 1875. You can make money on older houses, but you must understand the level of repairs and budget extra money for the unknowns.

What problems can you run into when repairing old houses?

With a newer house, you can run into problems when doing a rehab, but a newer house usually has a decent furnace, plumbing system, electrical system, and foundation. With older houses, you never know what you are going to find nor do you know how much a rehab will cost until it is complete.

I have an active flip that needed the interior walls stripped because the plaster was crumbling. Drywall replacement is not a huge deal because you can figure exactly how many sheets you need and calculate the labor costs. The problem is you do not know what you will find behind the walls. In this house, the wiring was spliced without junction boxes. This was a huge code violation and fire hazard. We had to rewire almost the entire house.

This was not the only problem we found after the rehab began. The roof appeared to be questionable and we planned to replace it. However, when my contractor started tearing off the shingles, he found four layers! The previous roofer had covered up the layers by raising the fascia so that only one layer of shingles showed. This discovery was not a disaster, but it did add to the labor and disposal costs.

Why do old houses always have uneven floors?

Nothing scares away a buyer faster than a house they think might have structural problems. Uneven floors may or may not be a serious problem, but they will scare off most buyers. Many issues can cause uneven floors: settling ground, rotten floor joists, crumbling foundation, or poor construction. Usually, an uneven floor can be leveled easily with more support and bracing. Houses settle all the time, and over the course of 100 years, a lot of settling can occur.

The problem with uneven floors is you do not always know the cause of the problem because you cannot get under the floor. Some old houses have basements, some have crawl spaces, and some have nothing. I have bought multiple houses that had neither a crawl space nor access to the space below the floors and required a flooring tear out. Before you buy a house, you cannot exactly tear up the flooring during an inspection. I had to take a chance and hope the uneven floors were due to a minor, unseen problem. Luckily, in most cases the ground had settled, meaning it could be easily fixed by adjusting the floor supports.

49

How can you tell if an old house has foundation problems?

One of the scariest repairs for any house is a repair to a faulty foundation. If you do not take care of it soon enough, a foundation problem can destroy a house. If the foundation is bad, there are usually signs: uneven floors, cracks in the walls, and cracks in the foundation. Hairline cracks are usually not a big deal and are common. Cracks that are more than one-fourth of an inch wide or are offset by more than one-fourth of an inch can indicate major problems. Water seeping through the foundation can indicate major problems. One of my flips has water seeping through the foundation, and my contractor is working to figure out the best way to repair it. He is either going to have to pour new foundation walls or dig out the ground around the outside, reseal, and repair the foundation. Whatever route he takes will be expensive!

If you think a house you are interested in has a foundation problem, get a professional to inspect it! Pouring a new foundation is not easy and sometimes not possible. Foundation repairs could cost anywhere from $2,000 to $25,000. In some rare cases, you must lift the house off the old foundation and pour a new one.

Plumbing problems in old houses

You must replace the galvanized pipes in many old houses. Galvanized pipes corrode over time and impair the quality of the drinking water. New plumbing technology has reduced the cost of pipe replacement since you no longer need to use expensive copper. However, replacing the plumbing in a house will costs thousands of dollars, and the biggest problems are found in houses with a finished basement. If a basement is finished, you must tear up the drywall to access the plumbing, which will add more costs. It is always a good idea to have the plumbing system thoroughly checked in any house you buy, especially if it's an older house.

Other issues to look out for

Old houses were originally built with plaster, not sheets of drywall like in newer houses. Plaster is much harder to work with than drywall. In fact, many contractors do not even know how to work with or patch plaster. If you either have cracks in the plaster or crumbling plaster, it is usually better to replace it all with drywall than to repair it. When you replace plaster, you may find electrical problems or you may discover the house has no insulation. You may even find some of the studs are rotting or have been cut at some point and are not supporting the house as well as they should. I have discovered these issues in older houses. I think I should still make a profit on these flips, but you must account for the extra repair costs that come with an older house.

Is an older house better for a fix and flip or a rental property?

When I buy rental properties, I have very strict criteria, and one is the age of the house. I try not to buy any rental property built before 1960. I like newer rental properties because I will hold them for a very long time. My rentals provide great cash flow, and I do not plan to sell them any time soon. The older the house, the more likely a major problem will come up during ownership. I would rather flip an older house than hold it as a rental because the property will become someone else's responsibility. I still try to repair the flip as much as I can, and I do not hide any problems. However, with old houses, you will to have to make more repairs. That is why my cash flow calculator for rental properties has a higher maintenance allocation than it does for an older a house.

How much extra should you budget for repairs on an older house?

When I plan a rehab, I generally add an extra 20 percent to the cost of repairs, and I frequently end up spending that money on something unexpected. On older houses, I assume there is going to be an extra 30 percent in repairs needed above what I plan for. Not every house will need that much work, but some will need more and some less. I will not stop buying old houses, but I will make sure I have plenty of room for potential unknowns.

10. How and Why I Lost Money on a Flip

I have a lot of experience and knowledge about flipping. However, even with that experience, I can still lose money. In fact, I have lost money on a few flips that initially looked like great deals. It does not feel good to lose money on a flip, and I would rather not talk about it, but I know telling this story will help others.

Multiple factors caused me to lose money on this flip. I probably paid a little too much for the house; I did not plan all the repairs as accurately as I should have; and multiple unanticipated issues arose.

How much money did I lose?

To be perfectly honest, I did not suffer a net loss because I am a real estate agent. I did lose money on paper when you factor out the commissions I earned when I bought and sold the property. I earned a three percent commission when I bought the house, and I paid myself a two percent commission when I sold it. After all the expenses and surprises, I ended up losing $762, not counting the commissions.

I bought the house for $140,403 and made $4,212 in commission on the purchase. I sold the house for $192,000 and paid myself a $3,840 commission on the sale. I actually made $7,310 on the property if you count my agent duties, but on the flip portion, I lost money. I do account for the commissions I earn when I buy a flip, but I was planning to make at least $25,000 on this property, not $7,300!

How did I buy this property?

I bought this house as a short sale. It was on the market for $140,000, and I made an immediate offer for full price and waited to hear back. I knew the house would be worth close to $200,000 and did not need too much work (or so I thought). After I made my offer, I was informed that the seller had received multiple offers, and I needed to send in my highest-and-best offer.

I raised my offer to $140,403 and waited again. For my highest-and-best offers, I like to use odd numbers because I want to beat out someone who has the same idea as me but may offer a round number like $140,000. I was informed that the seller had accepted my offer, and I had to wait to see if the bank would accept my offer since, in a short sale situation, the bank must approve all offers.

Three months later, the bank accepted my offer and we closed on the house!

I used a brand-new contractor on this flip

After I went under contract and bought the house, I ended up buying two more flips and getting a couple more properties under contract. Also, two months before this purchase, I had a falling out with a contractor I had used for years. I had to look for new contractors, and after interviewing quite a few, I decided to try one I found on Angie's List.

The house needed paint, carpet, electrical work, windows, some kitchen work, a new bath, lots of yard cleanup, and some work in the basement. The contractor bid a little over $18,000 for everything, and I thought that was a fair price. He also said it would take him about a month to complete the work. It always takes contractors longer to do the work than they say it will!

How long did it actually take to complete the work?

The contractor I used did a good job and stayed mostly on budget. We made a few changes that added to the costs, but it took almost three months to complete the work. The final repair bill was just over $20,000, and we put the house on the market in November. It took five months because I did not have my contractor start until a couple of months after I bought it. I was so busy with trying to get my other flips ready to sell that it took me too long to get work started on this one.

What unexpected costs came up during the inspection?

I listed the house for $204,900 and did not get an offer the first three weeks. I lowered the price to $199,900 and received an offer a few weeks later for $185,000. We negotiated a sale price of $192,000. I usually sell my flips much quicker and do not have to lower the price, but this house had a few negatives.

- The one-car garage was converted to a bedroom, and I think many people wanted a garage.
- The house had a strange floor plan considering the converted garage, and although it had more square feet than many higher-priced comps, the house felt chopped up and small.

Everything fell apart during the inspection, at least on my end. The buyers asked for a roof inspection and for the furnace to be replaced, and they learned the house is on a septic system! I should have had the roof and furnace checked, but my other contractors usually looked at those items for me. I assumed they were okay since the new contractor did not mention them, and he said he had roofing and HVAC experience. The roof and a new furnace ended up costing another $7,500.

The septic system was a total shock to me. When I bought the house, it was listed as being on a sewer system, and the previous four listings in MLS showed a sewer system as well. The buyer had it scoped and saw the sewer line drained right into a septic tank. We had a septic company look at it, and it turned out the line drained into a septic tank and then the septic tank drained to the city sewer! We had to dig up the yard and put in a line that bypassed the septic tank and connected to the city sewer. Luckily, the city was very cool about the situation and worked with us to get things connected correctly. That sewer line ended up costing about $4,000.

What were the total costs?

Even though I bought the house for $140,403 and sold it for $192,000, I made very little on the flip. I only made the money I did because I am a real estate agent and profited on the commissions.

Estimated Repairs:	$18,000
Actual Repairs:	$31,500
Estimated Selling Costs:	$10,600
Actual Selling Costs:	$10,600
Estimated interest:	$3,000
Actual Interest:	$3,500
Estimated Carrying Costs:	$3,000
Actual Carrying Costs:	$4,300
Buying Costs:	$2,800
Total Estimated:	**$36,600**
Total Costs:	**$52,700**

My interest and carrying costs increased because I held the property longer than I anticipated. During that time, I had to pay more taxes, more insurance, and more utilities. Not only did I have more costs than expected, I also sold the house for less than I projected. This is why it is so important to leave yourself enough profit margins on flips to cover the unexpected.

Conclusion

Things rarely go as planned when you flip houses, and this property had many problems. I still managed to profit a bit, but if I were not an agent, I would have lost money.

11. The Top 10 Mistakes New Flippers Make

Flipping houses can be a very lucrative business, but it is not easy to get started. House flipping is often glamorized by television and companies trying to sell training programs. Television and real estate investing gurus make flipping look easy, though there is so much more involved than what they show you. If you learn some of the most common mistakes to avoid, it can be a lot of fun and a great source of income. If you happen to make some of the following mistakes, they'll hopefully be a learning experience and help you improve your business. House flipping is not a get-rich-quick business, and it can take time to build it up. Here are a few mistakes either I or others have made over the years.

1. Thinking that house flipping is as easy as it looks on television

On most house-flipping shows, they show flippers making a lot of money in a very short period of time. The problem with these shows is they make the process look much more profitable than it actually is. They often forget to mention these costs:

Selling costs: You must pay real estate agents, closing companies or attorneys, title fees, transfer taxes, recording fees, and other costs.

Carrying costs: While you own the house, you must pay property taxes, insurance, HOA dues, utilities, maintenance costs (lawn, snow removal), etc.

Financing costs: Few flippers have the cash to buy without a loan, especially if they are doing multiple deals at once. Some flippers will be able to obtain bank loans and others will have to use hard money. The financing costs can be as much as 3 to 10 percent of the cost of the house.

Buying costs: When you buy a house, you may have to pay for the appraisal, inspection, closing and recording fees and more.

These costs can easily add 10 to 20 percent of the selling price to the budget. When flippers buy a property for $100,000, put $30,000 of work into it, and sell it for $200,000, they do not make $70,000. They most likely make $40,000 or less once all costs are accounted for.

House-flipping shows also depict the flippers doing their own remodel, which does not happen in the real world and is another mistake flippers make. Selling a flip also usually takes much longer than the shows portray.

2. Doing the work yourself

Another huge mistake flippers make is remodeling the house themselves. I made this mistake on a flip I bought in 2006. I thought I would save money on labor by working on the house and avoiding hiring a contractor. Doing the work myself cost me more money than hiring a contractor because it took me so long.

I thought it would take me a couple of months to finish the work on this flip, and instead it took me over 6 months. Because flipping carrying costs are so high, any savings from labor were gone. I also did not do a great job with some of my repairs and had to have a contractor come in to make sure I did things right. The worst part was the stress it put on me to finish the stupid house. I also missed out on many work opportunities because I spent so much time working on the house. My time is much more valuably spent finding deals, managing the contractors, or working on my business than doing manual labor. Yes, you see TV flippers doing the work themselves, but that is all for show. I have talked to one of them, and the producers had him lay tile for television. He had never laid tile before and it all had to be torn out when he was done. Just because they are doing it on television does not mean it is a good idea.

3. Counting on house prices to keep rising to make a profit

I am located in Colorado, and we have a crazy market right now. We have one of the highest appreciation rates in the country, and that can make it tough to find deals. On some properties I flipped over the last two years, I made much more money than I thought because prices have been rising. However, rising prices can get flippers into trouble. Some people will assume prices will keep going up and base how much they pay for a flip on the future value. This strategy is what caused many flippers to go bankrupt during the housing crisis. They bought houses assuming the market would keep going up, and when the market changed, they lost everything. I flipped houses before, during, and after the housing market crash. I never bought a flip assuming it would be worth more than the current market value when I sold it. This strategy has worked well, and I will continue to use it.

4. Partnering with the wrong people

Many house flippers will partner with another investor. In many cases, one investor will provide the money and another investor will find the deals and do most of the work. Partnering can work out great in real estate if everyone's job is clear and it is all in writing. I see other real estate investors partnering on flips because they want to share the risk. They do not have a clear job description for what each partner is responsible for or a clear definition of who pays what and when. Many times, the partners have different ideas of what hard work is or how much time should be spent on the project. When problems come up, there is no clear exit solution.

It is usually not smart to partner on a deal if you're looking just to feel safe and share the risk. The best partnerships result from partners who have clearly defined roles and bring different skills to the project.

5. Hiring the wrong contractors or not keeping track of contractors

One of the biggest challenges to running a flipping business is hiring the right contractors and keeping them working. It is tough to find decent contractors, and when you do find decent ones, many times they don't stay decent. They will raise prices, take on too many jobs, hire the wrong people, or get tired of the business. We must keep tabs on our contractors to make sure they are working fast and within budget. If we don't check on a house or a contractor for a week or two, I can almost guarantee they aren't doing what they are supposed to. We are in constant contact with our contractors and are always looking for more as well.

When you do not check on a house or the contractor, there is a better chance they will rip you off. Try not to pay too much money upfront to new contractors and make sure you keep close tabs on the work they have done before you pay them more. Additionally, get multiple bids from different contractors. There can be a huge price difference between contractors.

6. Underestimating the time it takes

Another mistake I see house flippers make is assuming it will only take a couple of months to buy a house, fix it up, and sell it. In reality, I would not count on a flip taking less than 6 months. Here is why it takes so long:

61

- **Getting the work done**: When you buy a house, the contractor you use probably cannot start work right away. They may be a week or two away from starting while they finish other jobs. When they do start, you must decide what to fix and how much to pay. This all assumes you have a contractor lined up and ready to go. Many new flippers buy a house and then start looking for a contractor. It can take from 1 to 3 months to get the work done, depending on the property's condition. Once the house is repaired, you usually need to do a walk-through with the contractor and have him fix mistakes. Then the house must be cleaned prior to listing.

- **Getting the house listed and under contract**: It can take a few days or longer to get a house listed. You should take great pictures, have an agent list it for you, and possibly stage it. Once it's listed, it may take anywhere from 1 to 90 days to get the house under contract ,depending on your market. Our houses typically go under contract within 3 to 4 weeks in a normal market, but recently it's taken less than a week in our crazy market.

- **Getting the house closed.** Once the house is under contract, it can take anywhere from 30 to 60 days to close the deal. Lenders are taking longer and longer to close on houses. We usually sell to owner occupants, and it is common for the escrow process to take 45 days if nothing goes wrong. There is the chance a contract could fall through due to inspection problems or financing problems.

If everything goes well with the contractor, the listing, and the sale, it could take as little as 3 months to sell a flip. But that is usually the best-case scenario. If the work takes longer, the house does not sell right away, or a contract falls apart, it could easily take six months. It is very important for investors to count on the home taking longer to sell than they think because the costs build very quickly the longer you own a property.

7. Underestimating the cost of repairs

Another difficult part of flipping houses is knowing what repairs will cost. I have been repairing houses (or having contractors repair them) for over 15 years. I have a pretty good idea of repair costs, but even I can be wrong. When I come up with a budget or get a bid from a contractor, I always add about 15 to 20 percent to that bid to account for unexpected costs. There are almost always repairs that pop up—repairs you did not think about or know of when you bought the house. If you are trying to estimate costs without any experience and without help from a contractor, it can be a disaster.

8. Taking on too big of a project for your first flip

I have flipped houses that needed close to $100,000 in repairs. One house needed new stucco, a new well, electric, plumbing, windows, doors, kitchen, bath, drywall, foundation, insulation, landscaping, heating system, flooring, paint, and more. Not only does it take a lot of money to flip a house that needs a lot of work, but it also takes longer. It can be harder to find contractors who will do the job, and much more can go wrong. Some of my biggest flipping mistakes were from buying houses that needed too much work.

9. Paying over $30,000 to learn how to invest in real estate

There are many mentoring programs for real estate investors. Some are great and others are giant marketing ploys meant to take as much money as possible from unsuspecting investors. When you hear ads on the radio for a free house-flipping seminar or workshop, be wary, even if it's taught by a popular house flipper. House flipping is not easy, even though they make it seem that way. These companies pay television house flippers to endorse their program, but the person you are familiar with is not teaching the classes. The course is usually taught by beginning flippers or people who have never flipped at all.

The programs draw you in with a free seminar, then say you need a 3-day workshop to learn the secrets. Finally, they try to suck you into a $30,000 mentoring program to show you how to really flip. Save your money and buy a house instead.

10. Not knowing the value of the house or overpricing a house

The most important thing to know when flipping a house is the selling price after repairs. If you think your flip is worth $10,000 more than it is, it will throw everything else off. You must know your values and know them very well. The best person to help value your house is a real estate agent. Zillow gives values, but they can be as much as 20 percent off. You can look at houses for sale in the neighborhood, but that does not mean they are actually selling for that price.

If you over-estimate the value or price a house too high, it will cost you money. Houses that are priced too high sit on the market and end up selling for less money than if they were priced correctly. I see some flippers price houses too high because they are trying to make up for other costs being too

64

high (repairs, carrying costs, selling costs). When you price a house too high, it does not fix mistakes you made on the flip. It makes it all worse. The longer you hold the property, the more costs you will have and the less the house will sell for.

Conclusion

Flipping houses is fun, and you can make a lot of money, but it is not as easy as some make it out to be. House-flipping shows leave a lot of the details out, and house-flipping gurus will not give you $30,000 of value. The best way to learn to flip houses is to educate yourself with books, learn from other investors, and do a lot of homework. Many successful flippers will not make much on their first flip. I have interviewed quite a few who lost money on their first deal. Just like any business, it takes time to learn the best practices and find success.

Part 3: How Do You Know What Houses Can Be Flipped?

12. How to Determine Whether to Fix and Flip or Buy and Hold a Property

One of the most common questions I hear is, "How do I determine whether to fix and flip or buy and hold a property as a long-term rental?" Many people may find it easier to find a rental property than to find a fix and flip, but I find it harder to locate rental properties. I have very strict guidelines that my rental properties must meet: cash flow, cash on cash return, location, condition, age, and more. I consider all these things when buying a rental. With flips, I want to make sure I can sell the house for a profit in less than six months, and I am not worried about the location, cash flow, or cash on cash return as much.

Why is my buying strategy so strict on long-term rentals?

It is easier for me to find a property to flip because I have such strict buying criteria on my rentals. I buy my rental properties based on cash flow, and I assume I will hold them for many years, if not forever. I want to make sure my rentals are great properties that will be easy to manage. I am very meticulous about the location, condition, and age because I am holding these properties so long.

How does location affect whether I will fix and flip or buy and hold a property?

I primarily buy fix and flips within a 40-mile radius of my location. I buy rental properties within 10 miles of where I live, although I prefer them to be much closer. The reason I buy flips further away is because I am selling them quickly, and I am only concerned with whether they will sell and for how much. With rental properties, I need to think about the long-term prospects of the area I am buying in, the future economy, and the rental market.

I also buy many fix and flips in small towns populated with fewer than 5,000 people. Because I am a real estate agent, it is easy for me to determine house values. Figuring rental rates is much tougher, especially in small towns. Since the small towns are farther away and have less certainty in the rental market, I do not buy rentals in them.

How does the age of the home determine whether I will fix and flip or hold a property?

I prefer houses that are less than ten years old for my rental properties. The newer the house, the less maintenance and repairs it will need. Finding great rentals that are less than ten years old is not easy, and most of my rentals are about 30 to 40 years old. I try to stay away from any rental properties that are older than 50 years.

I tend to be very cautious when considering 100-year-old houses for rental properties. The older a house is, the greater the chance that it will need major work at some point. I am also cautious when buying old houses for fix and flips, but I will not be holding a fix and flip for years. Since I sell fix-and-flip properties quickly, there is less of a chance I will run into a major problem with them than with long-term rentals.

How does the amount of work needed on a house determine if I will fix and flip or buy and hold?

I buy every house below market value. You cannot fix and flip without getting a great deal, and it is hard to get great cash flow without a great deal as well. Buying a house below market value usually means the house needs work.

If a house needs a lot of work, a new kitchen, new baths, carpet, paint, a roof, etc., it can cost $20,000 to $30,000…or more. I may have $50,000 or more into a rental property because I am already putting 20 percent down and adding $30,000 in repairs. Having that much cash into a rental will lower my cash on cash returns and limit my ability to buy more rental properties.

I prefer that my rental properties need as few repairs as possible. On my fix-and-flip properties, I also like to limit the repairs needed, but it is not as big of an issue. It costs more to make repairs on a fix and flip, but when I sell the house, I will get that cash back. With a rental property, that cash is locked up until I refinance it.

How do rent-to-value ratios affect whether I fix and flip or buy and hold?

Some neighborhoods have great rent-to-value ratios. The rent-to-value ratio is the amount the house will rent for compared to what I must pay for it. I am lucky that the rent-to-value ratios in my town are better than in surrounding towns. There is also a sweet spot for rent-to-value ratios in the $80,000 to $150,000 range. Most of my fix and flips are not in my town, even though I would love them to be! Because I live in a bigger town, there is more demand for houses and fewer great deals. Most of my flips are in other towns that have less favorable rent-to-value ratios.

Conclusion

Even though long-term rentals provide a better investment over time, I still do many fix and flips to generate income. I actually use much of the income from my fix and flips to purchase long-term rentals. To have the success I have had with my rental properties, I must be very cautious about what I buy. Looking at the numbers on my rental properties, I could fix and flip many of them and make a profit, but I will make much more by keeping them as rentals.

13. Is It better to Fix and Flip Houses or Buy and Hold Rental Properties?

I consider many factors when I determine whether to flip or hold, but believe it or not, I have much stricter criteria for my rentals than for my fix and flips.

I first wrote this chapter just after purchasing my seventh long-term rental property. I purchased this house in April of 2013 and paid $113,000. I estimated the ARV (after repaired value) to be $160,000 to $165,000. This article will discuss this particular property, and although I could have flipped this house, I chose to keep it as a rental.

There is plenty of room to fix and flip rental property number seven, but I am choosing to keep it as a long-term rental. I do many flips, and they are a large part of my income, but income alone will not make me wealthy. Long-term rental properties are what I am counting on to make me wealthy because they offer passive income.

What is the financing cost of a fix and flip compared to a rental property?

If you do not have the cash to buy a fix and flip, short-term financing can be expensive. Average hard-money lenders may charge 10 to 15 percent interest plus 2 to 4 percent in upfront points on the purchase price of a house. It is much easier and less expensive to get long-term financing on a rental property than on a fix and flip. Banks like long-term loans because they will receive interest for years. With fix and flips, banks do not earn interest for nearly as long as they do with long-term rentals, so they charge higher interest and more fees.

What repairs are needed on a fix and flip versus a rental property?

To earn top-dollar returns, flips must have top-notch repairs. Renters can be much less fussy about houses because they don't own the house. Renters are not worried about furnaces, roofs, plumbing, and the house's bare-bones structure because if anything breaks, they are not responsible. On a flip, the buyers pay a lot of money for a house they will own for years. They will get an inspection and make sure that everything works properly and that repairs have been done correctly. By no means am I suggesting a property owner should skimp on repairs, but there are certain things that you may not need to repair right away on a rental that you will need to repair on a flip.

What are the holding costs on a fix and flip versus a long-term rental?

Holding costs are higher on a fix and flip because it usually takes longer to sell a house than it does to rent it out. Many times, when you rent out a house, a renter is ready to move in immediately and will pay you rent and the deposit right away. If you are selling the house, it may take a month or two before an acceptable offer comes in, and then you must wait for the buyer to get their loan, complete inspections, etc. It can easily take three months or more for the flip to sell after you repair it and put it on the market. Every day the house sits vacant, the owner pays interest to the bank or hard-money lender and loses profits.

What are the costs associated with a fix and flip versus a rental property?

A flip generally has many more costs associated with it versus a rental. When selling a house, you must pay a real estate commission to the selling agent. We pay three percent commission to agents who sell our houses. We do not have to pay a listing commission because we are agents ourselves, but a non-agent would have to pay that as well. You also must pay title insurance, recording fees, closing fees, and—sometimes—buyer closing costs, which can amount to another three percent of the selling price.

Selling costs for a fix and flip may be ten percent or more of the sales price. If I keep the house as a long-term rental, I am not getting the instant profit of a flip, but I am also not giving up that ten percent.

Long-term income from a rental property vs. the instant profit of a flip

With a long-term rental, I continue to receive monthly cash flow while I own the house. I can also refinance the house after I have owned it a year and take cash out. The longer I own the house, the better the chances the house will appreciate. I also can charge higher rents and reduce the mortgage amount. If I can put off the instant gratification of the income from a flip, I will ultimately make much more from a rental.

Fix and flip profit vs. buy-and-hold income with rental property number seven

Here is my profit potential if I were to flip long-term rental number seven. I use rounded numbers to make the math simple. And remember, I am an agent, so I have fewer costs. To make this simpler, I will assume we are paying cash on the flip.

Repair costs:	$15,000
Utilities, insurance, and taxes:	$2,000
Real estate commission on $160,000 selling price:	$4,800
Title insurance, closing fees, and recording fees:	$1,500
Three percent buyer's closing costs:	$4,800
Total costs:	**$28,100**
Selling price $160,000 minus $113,000:	$47,000
Profit:	**$19,000**

A $19,000 profit is not bad, but that does not include loan costs, which would add at least $5,000 after paying interest and points. The figures also only include three percent for commissions because I am an agent.

If I were to hold rental property number seven instead, my costs will be much different. After I rent it, I will have about $34,500 cash into the house and cash flow of $500 per month. That is income of $6,000 per year. It would take just over three years for me to realize the same returns as the flip. I still have all the equity I had with the flip, and I am paying down my mortgage every month. I also do not have to pay as much tax because I can depreciate the home as a rental property.

Conclusion

My plan is to hold this property for the long term. I will keep bringing in more income every year as I pay the mortgage down and build equity as it appreciates. With enough long-term rental properties, the income becomes very significant. With the flip, I realize $19,000 in profit before taxes, and that's it. I must keep finding, fixing, and selling more properties to make more profit. On the other hand, the rental provides a continuous, yearly income source.

Even though I love rentals and the passive income they provide, I also love flipping because of the income. I can buy many more rentals because I am flipping houses. Some houses do not work as well for rentals as they do for flips either. In an ideal world, I would have hundreds of rentals that make me hundreds of thousands of dollars a month, but I must get there somehow!

To learn more about rentals, check out my book: Build a Rental Property Empire.

14. What Is the 70 Percent Rule?

The 70 percent rule is a common term used among many real estate investors. Do not feel bad if you do not know what it means. I had never heard of it until a few years ago when I had already flipped over 100 houses. The 70 percent rule is a way to figure out how much money you should pay for a flip. Even though I did not know what the 70 percent rule was, when I calculated what I pay for fix and flips, it came very close to the 70 percent rule.

What is the 70 percent rule?

The 70 percent rule states that an investor should pay 70 percent of the ARV (after repaired value) of a property minus the repairs needed.

If a house's ARV is $150,000 and it needs $25,000 in repairs, the 70 percent rule states an investor should pay $80,000 for it ($150,000 x 70 percent − $25,000 = $80,000). Buying a house for $80,000 that will be worth $150,000 may seem like an awesome deal, but you must account for all the costs involved in a flip.

Do I use the 70 percent rule when fixing and flipping?

I rarely use the 70 percent rule when deciding on a fix and flip. I like to write down all the numbers and decide on a deal after seeing my profit potential. On the above deal, I would write down all my costs and see if the profit potential was worth the risk. Occasionally, I will use the 70 percent rule to see how my numbers match up, and I am usually very close to what the 70 percent rule estimates.

How close would my purchase price be compared to the 70 percent rule?

$150,000 is the value of the house after the repairs, and it needs $25,000 in repairs. I always add an unknown-cost cushion of at least 10 percent. Selling the house would cost me approximately $6,500, which includes three percent commission, title insurance, and other closing fees. I will have insurance, utilities, and lawn maintenance while owning the house. I estimate those costs at $2,500. My financing costs will be about $3,500 with my bank's terms and loan costs. My selling costs are going to be lower than most people because I am a real estate agent and do not have to pay a listing agent.

$150,000	(ARV)
- 25,000	(repairs)
- 5,000	(unknown costs)
- 6,500	(selling costs)
- 2,500	(holding costs)
- 3,500	(loan costs)
= $107,500	(break-even point)

As you can see, when I subtract all my costs, I have a break-even point of $107,500. I usually want at least a $25,000 profit on my low-end fix and flips (under $125,000 purchase price). If I figure in a $25,000 profit, I should buy the property for $82,500. An investor who is not a real estate agent would be right at $80,000 or even a little lower because they would have to pay another three percent commission on the sales price.

How accurate is the 70 percent rule?

As you can see, based on my own calculations, the 70 percent rule was extremely close to what I would pay. In fact, my numbers on almost all my flips are right around the 70 percent rule. If I can get houses for less, that is great but difficult in this market. For beginner investors, I think the 70 percent rule is a great way to get an idea of what to pay for a flip. You must make sure your repair estimates are accurate for the rule to work.

Conclusion

The 70 percent rule is a great tool for investors. It provides an accurate purchase price for fix-and-flip investors, assuming the repairs and ARV are accurate. As an experienced flipper, I still write down all the costs on every house I consider. I think all investors should generally avoid relying on rules to make final decisions, but rules can help weed out properties that do not have enough profit margin.

15. How to Determine Market Value on Investment Properties

A huge key to my success is buying houses below market value, but how do you know what market value is? If you are not a real estate agent, it is very difficult—but possible—to determine fair-market value. If you are just beginning to invest in real estate, it is wise to use multiple ways to find market value.

When you are fixing and flipping houses, market value is obviously the most important factor for determining profit. Actually, ARV (after repaired value) is the most important factor because you want to know what the house will sell for when it is fixed.

What is the easiest way to determine market value?

The easiest way to determine market value is to hire a professional. I am an agent and provide comparative market evaluations for sellers all the time. I also provide values for investors and buyers. The trick for a new investor is convincing an agent that you are a serious investor who won't waste the agent's time. The easiest way to overcome this problem is to buy a house, but that is not realistic for a beginning investor who is trying to determine values.

My advice is to be perfectly honest with agents. Tell them you are new and you are trying to determine market values. It helps if you have done some work first and can ask them if the value you came up with seems accurate. Then, buy them lunch or give them something in return. Simple gestures like buying lunch can make a huge difference in convincing someone to help you.

Do not ask the agent for ridiculous things or make huge requests. Do not ask for 100 values or sales comps from the last two years for an entire town. I recently had an investor ask me for all the sold cash comps in the last year for metro Denver. Then he wanted me to put them all on an Excel spreadsheet and email them to him. I had never talked to this investor prior to this request, and I was just a little put off that he expected me to spend hours and hours of work for him. He gave me no reason to do this work and did not even tell me why he wanted this information. To top it all off, I am not even in the Denver market.

How to come up with a house value when you are not an agent

I mentioned that it would be good to have your own value in mind when talking to an agent. How do you come up with a value yourself? It is not easy to value a house unless you use a website like Zillow. However, Zillow is not always accurate. On my own properties, some of the values from Zillow were as much as 40 percent off! I would not trust Zillow to provide house values, although you can get some great information, like market trends, from Zillow.

When I value properties, I use sales comparables to determine values. I compare multiple sales in the last six months that are as similar as possible to the house I am valuing. As an agent, I can easily pull up any sold comps I want from the MLS. If you are not an agent, it is not so easy to find sold comps. You can find sold comps online at Zillow and a few other websites, but you will not get all the information you need.

Zillow uses all the sold comps it can find: foreclosures, short sales and sometimes trustee sales. This is important because you do not always know if those were market sales or just sales. A trustee sale price could simply be the amount the bank was owed and not a market sale. You also do not know what the condition was of the sale, what concessions were made, or the financing terms. You do not know how long a house was on the market, how many price changes there were, or if it was a short sale or an REO. You need these vital details to make an accurate valuation.

It is possible for a non-agent investor to determine a range of values based on online comps, but you still need to talk to an agent to make sure your values are accurate. If you have a great agent, they will probably offer you sold comps in an area and make your life much easier!

Using active comps to value properties

It is also possible to use active listings to value properties. It is not easy to use this method because an active listing does not mean it will sell for the asking price, if at all. Active comps do give you an idea of what is for sale in a neighborhood and what the competition is. I use active along with sold comps to value properties. You can use active comps for a broad value but not a solid value. The best way to use active comps for values is to track them over time. Keep track of the asking price, when they go under contract, and for how much they sell. When you know the history of a sale on a website like Zillow, that comp becomes much more valuable.

Adjusting for values

When you find sold and active comps that are similar to your subject, you still have more work to do. You must decide if you need to make adjustments for the differences between the comparables and the property that you are valuing. If you have a house with a one-car garage and the sales comps have two-car garages, you must make an adjustment. If the bedroom, bathroom, or room count is different, if square footage is different, views, location, or anything else is different, you need to make adjustments. Coming up with the adjustment is the tricky part. More expensive houses have different adjustments than less expensive ones. Different areas of the country put more value on certain amenities than other parts of the country. Here is an example of adjustments you might make:

- $5,000 per bedroom
- $30 per square foot
- $5,000 per garage space
- $4,000 per bathroom
- $20,000 for condition

Again, a real estate agent can help you figure out how much value various amenities add. When you look at enough houses and comparables, you should start to get an idea of how much value various features and size add. It will take time to get to know your market and be able to figure values and adjustments accurately.

Conclusion

If you aren't a real estate agent, it is not easy to come up with a value. If you can find an investor-friendly agent, it will save you a lot of time and trouble when determingin values. The best way to determine value is by looking at houses, checking out sold comps, and then comparing what you came up with to a real estate agent's value.

How Much Does It Cost to Fix Up a House?

Another important factor when choosing a property is what it will cost to repair. I fix up many houses, whether they are my personal house, my rental properties, or my fix and flips. When I repair a house, I don't mean I do the work myself; I have a contractor do it for me. The most difficult part about fixing up a house is finding a great contractor and estimating repair costs. Estimating repair costs is not easy, but this chapter will give you an idea of what to expect. Repair costs will vary based on the quality of products used, how much labor costs are in your area, and the contractor you use.

Why would you want to buy a house that needs to be fixed up?

Almost all the houses I buy need work, and some need a lot of work. I would love to buy houses that are in great condition, but I also want to buy houses that are a great deal. To get a great deal, you usually must buy houses that need some repairs because there are fewer buyers for those houses. When a house needs many repairs, most buyers may not be able to get a loan on that house. The fewer potential buyers for a house, the better the deal you can get. It also takes cash to make repairs, which further reduces the number of people who can buy houses that need work. Many people do not want the hassle of making repairs or finding a contractor to make the repairs, which further reduces the number of buyers.

Even if you buy a house that is in great shape, it will need work at some point. The fixtures may become outdated, the interior or exterior may need paint, and things may eventually break.

What does it cost to paint a house?

When I fix up a house, I always paint it and replace the floor coverings, unless those items were just done. The cost to paint a house has increased a lot the last few years because the cost of paint and labor costs has increased. My cost to paint the interior of a house is about $1.50 to $2.00 per square foot. It costs about $2,200 to paint the interior of a 1,500-square-foot house. That includes painting the trim white and the walls a different color like beige or gray.

It costs more to paint the exterior. The paint is more expensive, more prep work is needed, and the weather must be nice. Painting the exterior can run $3.00 per square foot or more depending on the complexity and condition of the house. If the paint is peeling, it will cost much more to scrape and prepare the surface for new paint. If a house has lead-based paint, the costs can be even higher due to the preparation and cleanup work needed to dispose of the old paint (another reason old houses are riskier). Your contractor or painter must be certified to remove lead-based paint, or they can face huge fines from the government. You only need to worry about lead paint on houses built prior to 1978.

How much does it cost to replace flooring?

When I replace the flooring, I usually use carpet for the living areas and vinyl or tile for the kitchens and bathrooms. If a house has hardwood, I will refinish the hardwood, but I do not add or replace hardwood due to the cost. It costs three times as much to install hardwood floors than to install carpet. Replacing the carpet in a 1,500-square-foot house will cost me $3,000 to $3,500. Vinyl or tile will cost another $500 to $1,000 for the kitchen and baths. These costs are for middle-of-the-road materials that look nice and will last but do not cost a fortune.

If a house already has hardwood, I will do my best to re-finish it because refinishing is cheaper than installing new carpet. I also like the look of hardwood floors, and buyers love them. I can re-finish a 1,500-square-foot house that is mostly hardwood for about $2,000.

We will sometimes install laminate flooring that looks like hardwood. We usually use it in our low-end flips because it is affordable and looks nice. We use slightly upgraded laminate, as the cheapest options do not look very good.

How much does it cost to replace fixtures?

Another great update is replacing the lights and plumbing fixtures. Brand new lights, door handles, and faucets that all match, can transform a house. I like to use oil-rubbed bronze, but we have also used brushed nickel. Light bedroom and bathroom light fixtures are as cheap as $10. You can buy a nice chandelier for under $150 as well as a nice ceiling fan. Door handles are $20 or less depending on the style, and faucets run from $35 to $150. For an entire house, you can replace the lights, door handles, and faucets for about $1,000 to $1,500.

How much does it cost to replace the appliances?

Another way to make a house look great is by adding new appliances. We put stainless steel appliances in our houses. I can get a stove for $500 to $600, a dishwasher for $300, and a microwave for $250. I usually do not buy a fridge for my flips. In our market, most houses are not sold with fridges, but you need to make sure that is the norm in your market. Appliances make a huge difference in the look of a kitchen, even if the cabinets are dated.

How much does it cost to cosmetically update a house?

If you do all the work mentioned above and the rest of the house is in decent shape, it will make a huge difference in the look and feel. I usually do all the repairs I discussed on every fix and flip. With my rentals, I usually do most of those repairs, but if a house is in decent condition, I can get away with less. Here are the total costs for a cosmetic upgrade on a 1,500-square-foot house:

New interior paint:	$2,200
New floor coverings:	$4,500
New fixtures:	$1,200
New appliances:	$1,300
Miscellaneous:	$3,000
Total cost:	**$12,200**

When you fix up a house, it almost always costs more than you think, so be prepared to spend more than what you calculate. It is very rare that I ever spend less than $10,000 on any house that I fix up because there are usually many little things that need repairing as well. Drywall holes, outlet covers, landscaping, and many more items will increase the costs. It is also rare that I do not have more major repairs to complete.

What do major repairs cost?

The repairs on my flips and rentals vary from basic cosmetics to a massive remodel. Here are other common repairs we make on houses and their costs.

Kitchens: It is not as expensive as you might think to replace a kitchen. I can replace a basic kitchen, including cabinets, counter tops, and sink for $4,000 in materials or less. After adding the labor, you can replace a kitchen for well under $8,000.

Baths: Baths can involve gut jobs or a simple vanity replacement. For a full gut job, I can usually get it done for less than $3,000. A vanity, toilet, and bath-surround can be replaced for less than $1,000.

Roof: I have a great roofer who will replace the roof on a 1,500-square-foot house for around $6,000.

Electrical: Electrical repairs can vary a great deal based on what needs to be done. Minor repairs can be a couple hundred dollars; major rewiring jobs can be $5,000. It is important to get any electrical concerns checked out to see how serious they are.

Plumbing: Plumbing is similar to electrical. A minor job can be very cheap, but re-plumbing a house can cost $5,000 or more.

Sewer: Sewer line replacements can be very expensive. Luckily, I have never had to replace one, but replacing a line can cost $3,000 to $15,000.

Foundation: Most foundation repairs are not fun to deal with. There are many issues, from settling, water leakage, grading issues, or structural problems. If you have water problems in the basement or crawl space, there may be a major foundation issue that costs $10,000 or more or a simple grading issue that some dirt work will fix.

Windows: Because we buy older houses all the time, we replace many windows. For basic vinyl windows, my contractors usually charge me about $300 per window materials and installation.

Doors: We also replace many interior doors. Six-panel white doors make a house look very nice. Doors are usually $100 to $150 per door installed.

Stucco and siding: I rarely replace the siding on a house, but I have on occasion. I am putting brand new stucco on a fix and flip that is costing about $8,500 for 1,250-square-foot. Replacing wood siding is cheaper, but you then must paint the wood siding. You can still re-side and paint a house for less than stucco in most cases ($5,000 to $7,000).

Drywall/Sheetrock: With old houses, I see a lot of plaster and bad drywall. Brand new drywall makes an old house look so much better than uneven crumbling plaster. On a recent flip, a drywall specialist charged about $5,000 for walls and ceilings that totaled about 1,200 square feet.

Furnace/hot water heater: I had a brand new forced-air furnace system installed for about $7,000 this year. To replace just the furnace costs about $2,500, air conditioning $3,000 and a hot water heater about $800.

How much do I spend on my remodels?

On my most recent fix and flip that is about to be put up for sale, I spent about $18,000 on the remodel. That included interior and exterior paint, new carpet, new doors, new trim, some electrical work, some new drywall, trash-out, landscaping work, and many little fixes. On one flip that is about to have the work started, I will spend over $50,000 on repairs. That house needs new plumbing, new electric, new paint everywhere, siding work, new windows, new doors, new drywall, new baths, new kitchen, new floors, new fixtures, new trim, and more.

Where do I buy repair and rehab materials?

I shop at Home Depot for most materials, including fixtures, doors, windows, door handles, and all the little stuff. We have a managed pro account, which offers huge discounts. I am also a member of the local real estate investors association, and as a result, get 2 percent off everything I buy from Home Depot. In 2017, we are on pace to spend over $1,000 a day at Home Depot!

Conclusion

Basic cosmetic repairs do not cost $50,000 or $100,000. I see kitchen remodels on television that cost $50,000, and I cannot believe my eyes or ears! Even if you use high-end materials like granite counters and custom cabinets, you should not spend $50,000 on a kitchen unless it is in a million-dollar house. I can always tell if someone is a beginning investor when they start talking about a basic remodel costing $50,000 or $75,000. Repairs can add up quickly on remodels, but not that quickly if you know what you are doing.

Remember, these costs are what I pay to fix up houses in my area. If you live in an expensive town, your costs may be significantly higher. Again, you would have much higher priced houses and materials as well. Different contractors also charge different rates and can make a huge difference on the repair costs.

16. Who Do You Listen to When Deciding What Houses to Flip?

There are many so-called experts in the real estate world, from late-night infomercial kings to your local real estate agent. Many people in the real estate field have vast knowledge and are an amazing resource, while others have no idea how to invest in real estate.

There are a lot of people who will try to convince you that real estate is a horrible investment. Many others will try to convince you to buy a $50,000 coaching program. There are others who will pretend to know what they are doing when they have no clue. You must be very careful who you listen to, and you must be cautious of who influences your decisions.

Should you let real estate gurus teach you about investing?

The first professional I want to discuss is the real estate guru. The real estate guru is the person selling a program that guarantees to make you a millionaire in 6 months, guarantees to find you properties for pennies on the dollar, and guarantees to show you a secret formula no one else knows about when investing in real estate.

The problem with real estate gurus is they don't make their money by investing in real estate. They make their money by selling overpriced real estate programs that don't work. Having said that, there are many seasoned investors who offer programs that work and teach people how to invest in real estate. How do you determine if the program you are looking at is legitimate or is from a guru trying to make a quick buck?

- **How much does the program cost, and how is the cost structured?** Most guru programs are very expensive, but many times the costs are hidden until you sign up. You may see an advertisement for a free seminar. Then, at the seminar, you must sign up for a workshop. At the workshop, you are offered one-on-one training, all with escalating costs. I have seen many programs charge $50,000 or more to teach about real estate investing.

- **Does the teacher have experience?** You want your teacher to have real estate investing experience. You want their experience to be as recent as possible, not from 20 years ago. The real estate world changes very quickly, and old strategies don't always work in the current lending and market conditions. Lending guidelines are constantly changing, and you want your coach to be an expert on investing in real estate in the current market. The real estate world has changed significantly in the last 5 years. The more recent the teacher's experience, the better.

- **The teacher should be willing to talk openly about their program and strategies.** If you ask a simple question, they should be able to answer you right away. If they dodge the question or make you buy their program to get the answer, watch out. A real teacher of real estate techniques wants to share their knowledge, help others, and get paid for their time and expertise. A guru will try to trick people into buying a program with fancy sales techniques and little useful information. If a teacher can't answer a simple question, they either don't have the knowledge or are trying to take you for every penny they can.

What are some good real estate coaching programs?

There are a lot of real estate coaches and websites. Some have a ton of great information, and some are just out to sell you stuff. There is nothing wrong with marketing and selling products if you are providing value. Not all sites are out to provide value, and you must be careful.

- Some real estate forums are full of great people and information. However, some forums have gotten so large that it is tough to know who to believe. Some members know what they are talking about, and others have no clue. When forums have over 200,000 members, it is very hard to differentiate between the good investors and the wannabees.
- J Scott is a very successful flipper. Look him up. He flips many houses each year and even wrote a book on the subject. J is always willing to help investors and gives away information all the time without charging a dime!
- I offer my own programs that focus on becoming a real estate investor and real estate agent. I don't spend a lot of time marketing these programs since I am still an active investor. But I do offer personal coaching in the form of conference calls and emails.

Local experts are the best teachers

Besides gurus and coaches, there are local experts who may be able to help you with investing strategies. There is also a good chance the local experts have no idea about how to invest in real estate. Agents and lenders are a great source of information for those looking to buy a house. However, most lenders and agents specialize in helping owner-occupied buyers, not investors. How do you know if a local expert can help you learn to invest?

Real estate agents who know investing

Real estate agents are trained to work with owner-occupied buyers. Our public schools don't teach us about investing in real estate, and real estate schools don't teach agents about investing in real estate either. If you aren't an agent yourself, which I highly suggest becoming, you need a great agent. Remember, unless you have a very savvy agent, the agent will know less about investing in real estate then you will.

I would estimate that 90 percent of real estate agents are not investing in real estate themselves and don't know how to invest in real estate. They don't know how much room an investor needs to flip a house. They do not know how to finance flips, and they do not know what repairs should cost. Make sure you are not taking bad flipping advice from agents.

Lenders who know about real estate investing

Lenders are trained to focus on getting buyers the lowest payments possible. Most lenders have no idea which loan options are available for flipping. You need to talk to a local lender in the bank's commercial department to determine if they offer flip loans.

Local REIA or local investors who know about investing

If you are looking for a local expert to help you learn the ropes, attend an REIA meetup. REIAs are clubs where investors share information and network. I highly suggest going to meetings, as you can learn a ton! Don't be intimidated, as many members have never done an investment deal themselves and are learning as well. You should be able to meet real investors doing deals in your area. Take them out to lunch and pick their brains. See how much information they will give you. Who knows, they may even need your help.

Legality of investing in real estate programs

I have heard many stories about people performing illegal acts because they learned illegal techniques from a real estate guru. It doesn't matter who taught you the illegal technique. If you are the one conduction the illegal activity, you are the one who will get into trouble. There is a very thin line regarding what can and cannot be done. Much of the confusion comes from whether someone needs a real estate license to perform certain duties. Please do your research on your own state's laws before you start investing in real estate.

There are some very common mistakes that people make when they begin investing in real estate. If you are trying to connect a buyer with the seller of a house for a fee, you need a real estate license. Many people like to start investing in real estate by wholesaling properties. To legally wholesale a home, you must have a legal title or a contract to buy the property. It is also illegal for agents to pay referral fees to unlicensed wholesalers in many states.

Conclusion

There are a lot of people trying to make money from real estate investing programs. I am trying to make a bit of money as well, both from my blog and from products and books I have published. J Scott, is a fantastic resource and will answer any questions you have, even if you don't buy his book. You will notice these people are very willing to give you plenty of free information, but they also put together programs with easy-to-understand legal techniques. If you have $50,000 to spend on a real estate guru's investing program, why not buy a house instead and learn through hands-on experience!

Part 4: How to Finance Fix and Flips

17. Should You Use Cash or a Loan to Flip?

It takes a lot of money to flip a house, and that is the biggest hurdle for most investors. Although there are ways to finance fix and flips, it is not as easy to get a loan for a flip as it is for a rental or personal residence. If you can get a loan on a flip, you will probably pay much higher rates than a you would for a regular mortgage. Is it worth it to pay these higher interest rates and loan costs?

How do I finance my fix and flips?

If I didn't finance them, there is no way I could handle so many simultaneous flips. However, my bank offers me a great deal with cheap financing. Here are my terms:

- Rate is prime plus two percent, which equals 5.25 percent
- One-year term
- 20 percent down payment on purchase price
- One percent origination fee
- No appraisal if the loan amount is less than $150,000
- 15- to 25-day closing depending on how busy my bank is

When I use bank financing, I must come up with the 20 percent down payment and the cash needed for repairs. If I buy a house for $100,000, my loan will be for $80,000. I would have to come up with down payment, repairs and carrying costs, which may amount to $50,000 or more. If I have seven simultaneous flips, I need at least $350,000 in cash invested in my flips. There are some cases where I must close on a house in 7 days or I cannot get a loan and must pay cash. So, in some cases, I will need even more available cash. That is why I also finance with private money and lines of credit.

I have a $120,000 line of credit on one of my paid-off rental properties and a $174,000 line of credit on my personal residence. I also borrow $160,000 from my sister, to whom I pay seven percent interest. On my lines of credit, I also pay prime plus two percent, which is currently 5.25 percent.

Although it may seem like I have a ton of cash available from my lines of credit and private-money lenders, it takes a lot of money to flip. On many of my most recent flips, I put more than 20 percent down to avoid an appraisal (for timing reasons). I have also had some flips require over $50,000 in repair costs.

What are other financing options?

It is rare to find fix-and-flip rates and fees as low as mine. Most banks charge much higher rates than those I pay (if they even offer flip financing). Even if a bank offers flip financing, they don't just give it to anyone. They want to lend to experienced flippers who have a track record of success and who they know and trust. I had a relationship with my lender for years while buying rentals before I approached them about financing flips. If you don't have a great local lender, there are other options.

Hard-Money Lenders: These lenders specialize in flips, and in some cases, will finance an entire deal. However, they also want to lend to experienced flippers and charge 10 to 16 percent interest in most cases.

Equity Partners: Some investors are willing to pay for a flip if they get a share of the profits. For example, the investor with the money pays for everything, and the other investor finds the

95

deal, does all the work, and sells the house. A typical split in this situation is 50/50.

Private Money: I already discussed how I obtain private money from my sister. Many flippers finance using private money. Most investors I have talked to pay a little higher interest rate than I do.

When you try to finance flips, you will find the rates are usually higher and the lenders want to see experienced flippers. The reason for the higher rates is the loan terms are much shorter and lenders make their money over long periods of time, not when they close the loan. There are also a lot of beginner flippers who have no idea what they are doing and are apt to lose money when they begin.

How much does the financing on a flip cost for a typical investor?

I won't use my numbers for financing flips because there are very few banks who will offer what mine does, and I have built up my relationships for years to get private money. If you can find money as cheap as mine, I think it is an easy decision to use it. But how much will the funding cost when you must use hard money or more expensive private money?

I will assume you can get a hard-money loan at 14 percent interest with 3 points. Each point equals one percent of the loan amount. With both hard money and private money, you can finance much more than 75 percent of the purchase price. In some cases, experienced flippers can finance the entire purchase amount and repairs. Here are what the financing costs would be in this scenario.

Purchase price:	$100,000
Repairs:	$30,000
Other costs (buying and carrying costs):	$5,000
Total cash needed:	$135,000
Hard money loan (90% of all costs):	$121,500
Cash needed after loan:	$13,500
Interest on loan (14 % for six months):	$8,505
Points paid (3% of $121,500):	$3,645
Total financing costs:	**$12,150**

There are many more costs when you use hard money or a more expensive private money lender. My average profit on a flip is more than $32,000 after all expenses. If I had to use hard money, my average profit would drop to $25,000. Even with that drop, I am going to show you why leverage is such an awesome tool while flipping—and while conducting most business—if used correctly.

Do you make more money flipping with cash or financing?

If you paid cash only, you would make $12,000 more than if you used a typical hard-money loan. Using only cash, my profit would jump from $32,000 to $37,000 on each deal. I would love to see $5,000 more on each flip. At that rate, I would make $60,000 more per year if I performed 12 flips. The problem is I could not flip 12 houses in one year using just cash.

Let's assume that, after flipping for a couple years and saving all after-tax profits, a flipper has $300,000 in cash. Who makes the most money? The investor who pays cash, the investor who uses a bank only, or the investor who uses hard money? For this example, let's assume our house has a purchase price of $100,00, needs $30,000 in repairs, includes $5,000 in carrying costs, and will sell for $185,000.

---	Cash Investor	Bank Investor Only	Hard Money
Cash needed:	$135,000	$60,000	$13,500
Loan amount:	0	$75,000	$121,500
Loan costs:	0	$4,000	$12,150
Selling costs:	$13,000	$13,000	$13,000
Repair cost:	$30,000	$30,000	$30,000
Carrying cost:	$5,000	$5,000	$5,000
Profit per deal:	**$37,000**	**$33,000**	**$24,850**
Deals done:	2	5	22
Total profit:	**$74,000**	**$165,000**	**$546,700**

Even though the cash investor makes more money per deal, the number of flips is lower than for an investor who uses financing. If you can still make money with higher financing costs, you can make a lot more money using leverage than if you only use cash. The cash investor can only buy two houses at a time, which severely limits the profit potential. The bank-only investor can buy five houses if they max out their available cash. The hard-money investor makes the most money because they can do the most deals. There will be many issues with doing 22 flips at once, like finding contractors, managing the timelines, and finding that many deals. Some hard-money lenders may also be hesitant to loan on that many houses at one time, but I know some who will.

What about investors who don't have a track record and can't get a hard-money or bank loan?

If you have never flipped a house, it is very hard to get started. No one wants to lend to someone who has no experience, but you need money to get experience. This is where partnerships come into play. Find someone with private money who will fund your deal, and offer to do all the work: finding the deal, managing repairs, selling the house, etc. Most private-money lenders won't want to lend to inexperienced investors at rates of 8, 10 or even 12 percent interest. However, they may be interested if they are an equity partner and get 50 percent of the profits. 50 percent may seem steep, but if you have no other choice, it is better than making nothing. Once you get a few deals under your belt and save some money, you can pursue the other financing options.

Conclusion

If you have the money to pay cash and are only interested in doing one flip at a time, maybe the best choice is to avoid financing. However, if you want to make a business out of flipping, the more leverage you can use, the more money you will make. You can also use more leverage with flips and apply your cash to other things like buying rental properties. With anything, you must be careful not to over-leverage yourself and sacrifice your buying criteria to get enough deals.

18. How to Finance Fix and Flips

One of the biggest hurdles to flipping is finding the money to do it. If you want to flip, you will need financing of some type, unless you have the cash lying around.

Unless you have more than four mortgages, it is not difficult to finance long-term rental properties. Banks like to finance properties that you are going to hold for the long-term. Banks do not like short-term loans because they make money on the interest paid on loans and stop making money as soon as you pay off the loan.

Most investors sell flips less than one year after buying them. This is a very short loan term for banks. To finance fix and flips, you must find short-term financing, which is usually much more expensive and harder to find.

You can use a long-term loan on a flip, but when you pay off that loan right away, the bank will start to ask questions. If they find you intended to flip that house and did not tell them, you probably will never get a loan from them again. If you want to flip multiple houses, you need to stay in good graces with your bank or whomever you get your money from, and that means being honest.

Does using a loan on my flips make it harder to buy properties?

Getting properties is tough in today's market. Using cash to make an offer usually will make your offer more appealing, but as you can see, I get loans on many of my flips.

Even though I am using financing to buy fix and flips, I write the offer as a cash deal. I can offer cash because I do not include any loan conditions or appraisal contingency in my offer. If I must pay cash, I can, but I can buy many more properties by getting a loan.

I include an additional-provisions paragraph that states: "I may get a portfolio loan instead of cash, but there will be no appraisal, no loan conditions, and I will pay cash if needed."

Most sellers accept my offer as cash, even though I usually get a loan on the property. I waive my inspection, appraisal, and loan conditions contingencies, which makes the offers just like cash.

19. How to Finance Fix and Flips with Hard Money

Many investors fund real estate deals using hard money as a short-term solution. Investors can use hard money to fund fix and flips or buy rental properties until they can secure long-term financing. Hard money is a great option for those who do not have the cash to flip a house themselves. However, there are many more costs associated with hard money.

What is hard money?

Hard money is a type of financing used to finance properties for a very short term (six months to a year). Hard-money lenders use much different terms than a traditional bank. These lenders get their money from investors, not from depositors like banks do. Hard-money lenders make their money by charging the end user (you) more than they must pay the investor who is loaning them the money.

They charge a very high interest rate. Most charge 10 to 16 percent (some drop rates below 10 percent for experienced flippers) as well as points for their money. One point equals one percent of the total loan, and costs can add up quickly when a hard-money lender charges 2, 3, or even 4 points on a loan.

Why would investors use hard money?

The advantage of a hard-money lender is they may loan more money than banks, and many banks will not even lend on flips. Most hard-money lenders base the amount of the loan on the ARV (after repaired value—how much the house will be worth once you fix it up). You may find they will loan 65 to 70 percent of ARV.

How a hard-money deal is structured

Here is an example of how one hard-money lender structures a deal. You buy a home for $60,000. The ARV is $130,000. The hard-money lender will loan up to 70 percent ARV on the property ($91,000). The hard-money lender requires bids or estimates for repairs and pays out the money for the repairs, similar to a construction loan. They will pay 25 percent of needed repairs at closing, and further payments will come in 25 percent increments as repairs are completed. The lender will not charge you any interest or points until you sell the home. Then, you pay them one large payment for the loan principle, interest, and points at the sale closing. This particular hard-money lender charges 15 percent interest and 4 points, but they will reduce the points you have to pay after you have done a few deals with them.

The costs to do a deal with a hard-money lender can add up very quickly. On this deal, if you use the money for six months, the interest will cost you $6,825, and the points will cost you $3,640. For investors who have no other options, using a hard-money lender can enable them to flip when they have no other options. There are also some hard-money lenders that charge lower rates.

Another lender I have worked with loaned me 85 percent of the purchase price and 100 percent of the repairs. They charged me 8.75 percent and 2.5 points. However, I have done over 120 flips, and I got the best deal they could offer. The rates and terms will vary greatly depending on your experience and how much money you put down.

Where can you find hard-money lenders?

There are many hard-money lenders out there. Many only lend in specific states, while some lend nationwide. The best way to find a hard-money lender is to search on any search engine for one in your state. If you want a few companies to talk to, send me an email: Mark@InvestFourMore.com, and I can send you updated information, including the one I work with.

Conclusion

I use a mix of traditional banks, lines of credit, and private money to fund my deals. I am fortunate that I have both the private money and cash available to complete many deals. I will usually use a bank loan for 80 percent of the purchase price, private money for the rest of the down payment, and my own money for repairs.

I have been doing this for over a decade, and that makes it much easier for me. If you need hard money, private money, or a partner to make things work, that should be your number one priority.

20. How to Use Private Money to Flip Houses

Private money has contributed greatly to my success, and it is also key to many other flippers' success. On my InvestFourMore Real Estate Podcast, I have interviewed many real estate investors, and many who flip houses use a lot of private money. It has been a recurring theme with almost every successful real estate flipper I talk to. Private money is an awesome tool because it gives the investor flexibility to close quickly, pay cash, and use less of their own money. The problem with private money is it is not easy to find! How can you find a private-money lender?

What is a private-money lender?

If you search for private-money lenders online, you will find many companies claiming to provide private money. The chances of finding a true private-money lender through a Google search is slim. Most companies claiming to be private-money lenders are actually hard-money lenders.

True private money comes from people who have a lot of cash and are willing to lend it to individual investors. Private money can come from friends, family, business partners, other real estate investors, or anyone with cash. It is not easy to ask for private money, and it is not easy to find people with money who are willing to lend it to individuals. Private money rates can vary from 0 percent (most likely a parent wanting to help their children) to 12 percent or higher, like hard money. The rates all depend on the lender's desired return, what the investor is willing to pay, and the risk involved.

Why is private money so important?

I use a mix of financing when I flip houses. I have 10 to 20 flips going at any one time, and in to do that many flips at once, I must have a lot of financing in place. I use these sources for private money:

- My sister lends me money that is secured against a couple of my rental properties. I pay her 7 percent per year and borrow the money year round.
- An investor who flips houses lends me money on individual deals at 10 to 11 percent and 2 points. He will finance the entire purchase price but none of the repairs.
- Another investor who used to flip lends me money on the same terms.
- I borrow money from my parents at 7 percent interest year round. I pay them much more than they would get if the money was sitting in a CD. They actually asked to invest in my business.

Some flippers will only use private money to fund their flipping business. When buying at a foreclosure auction, you may need cash within a couple of hours of winning the bid. Most banks or hard-money lenders cannot fund so quickly. Private-money lenders can fund deals right away, and they will have more-flexible terms than most banks and hard-money lenders. Banks and hard-money lenders will have certain lending guidelines. They will not want to lend over a certain amount of the purchase price or the After Repaired Value. Some private-money lenders will lend on the entire purchase price and all the repairs.

How can you find a private money lender?

Private money is very important to growing a flipping business, but it is not easy to find. As you can see, I use money from friends and family. I have no problem borrowing money from them since they are getting a great return and it helps my business as well. Here are the most common roadblocks to finding private money:

- Investors do not want to ask their friends or family because they are afraid of rejection or losing their money.
- Investors do not know anyone with a lot of cash.
- Investors do not have any experience flipping houses, and private-money lenders do not want to lend to them.

Overcoming any of these obstacles can be tough but not impossible. Here are some tips.

- If you are afraid of rejection, you are in the wrong business. It happens all the time in real estate, so don't worry about people saying no. It is not the end of the world. As for being afraid of losing money from people you know, you should also be worried about losing money from people you don't know! If you don't have confidence you can make money, maybe you need more education and experience.
- If you don't know anyone with a lot of cash, there are ways to find those people. First, you may know people with cash but have not thought about them or are afraid to ask them. Make a list of everyone you know and anyone they know or may have connections with.
- If you have never flipped a house, it is tough to get started. The best way to get attention from lenders is to find awesome deals. Find a deal that is so good that it is a no-brainer for the lender. Even if you screw up and can't pay back the loan, the lender could take the house back and still be in a good position.

I still don't know anyone with money. How do I find a private-money lender?

If you've reviewed all your contacts and still cannot find someone with money, you have more options. Investors lend flippers money all the time and are most likely doing it in your market. How do you find those lenders?

When someone is lent private money, a Deed of Trust is used to record the loan against the property. When a Deed of Trust is recorded against a property, it becomes public record, and anyone can see who the lender is. Look for properties that have been flipped (either sold recently or on the market), and check public records for private-money loans. As a real estate agent, I can look up public records on properties very easily and see what loans are against it. If I want to see the actual Deed of Trust, I can use the county's website or call the title company and ask for a copy. You can also use List Source to find properties with private-money loans against them.

With this technique, you can find investors who are lending to flippers in your market. Finding the investors who will lend money is just the first part of the process.

How do you convince someone to lend you money?

Once you find someone with money, you must convince them to lend it to you. The lender will realize advantages and disadvantages. You need to make sure you limit the disadvantages and make the advantages as big as possible. Make sure you think about the investor's perspective, not just yours.

Advantages for the investor looking to lend money:

- They will earn a higher rate of return than most investments like CDs, money market accounts, bonds, and possibly, the stock market.
- When you invest in stocks and bonds, you can lose your entire investment and have no collateral. When lending against real estate, your loan is secured against the property. If the borrower can't pay back the loan, the lender can foreclose on the property and take possession (assuming it is a first Deed of Trust).
- You know your exact return and when you will be paid back. With other investments, you are guessing what the returns may be and when.
- If the flipper knows what they are doing, they will buy very cheap houses. If the flipper defaults, the lender may actually make more money by taking possession of the house.

Disadvantages for the investor:

- The flipper may not be experienced. This could result in more costs than expected, the property being worth less than expected, the flip taking longer than expected, or other problems.
- The value of the property could decrease. This is usually only a problem when a flip takes a very long time to complete or the home is overpriced when the flipper tries to sell.
- It takes some work to foreclose on a property if the flipper defaults. The timeframes vary by state, but it could take a couple of months—or a couple of years in some extreme cases.

- If something goes wrong and the lender and flipper know each other, it could result in a lost friendship or family problems.

When trying to convince someone to lend you money, you must prove to them that their money is safe. You need to show them, with documentation, what the property is worth, what it will sell for, what repairs will be needed, what all the costs will be, and what the timeframe will be. Most new flippers underestimate most of these costs, and experienced investors will know if you are being unrealistic.

Don't be afraid to pay someone 10 percent interest or even more if needed. An investor will require high returns to take on the risk of private investing. The less experienced the flipper is, the more interest they will most likely have to pay. If there is not enough room in the flip to pay a higher interest rate and still make money, it is not a good deal.

Conclusion

Finding private money is not easy. The more experience you have, the easier it will be, and you may find private-money lenders coming to you. If you want to find and convince someone to lend you money, you need to have a great deal, prove you know what you are doing, and be willing to pay higher rates that most lenders require.

21. How to Find a Portfolio Lender Who Will Finance Multiple Investment Properties

A portfolio lender is crucial to many investors' strategy because they often lend on multiple investment properties. I have a great portfolio lender who allows me to finance as many properties as I want as long as I continue to qualify and have enough reserves. Having a good portfolio lender is extremely important to my strategy, which depends on buying many properties.

What is a portfolio lender and why are they important?

Many banks will not give you another mortgage if you already have four or more financed properties. There are some banks that will finance between four and ten properties, but they have many restrictions. Those restrictions include a 25 percent down payment and high credit scores. In addition, banks do not allow a cash-out refinance. Very few banks will give you a mortgage if you have ten or more financed properties. Most banks have restrictions on the number of mortgages they will give to one person because they sell their loans to institutional investors, and those investors only buy loans that conform to Fannie Mae guidelines.

A portfolio lender lends their own money and does not sell their loans to institutional investors. Because portfolio lenders do not have to conform to Fannie Mae guidelines, they will lend on more than four and even more than ten mortgages. They may also allow a cash-out refinance and are flexible with many other financing options, including flipping houses with short-term loans. Big banks will not loan to flippers for the most part.

What loans do portfolio lenders offer?

Since a portfolio lender is a local bank that loans their own money, they do not have to meet Fannie Mae lending guidelines, which allows them more flexibility. However, they do not offer all the loan programs that large banks offer. My portfolio lender does not offer a 30-year fixed mortgage. They only offer 15-year fixed, 5/30, or 7/30 ARM. To get the lowest interest rate, I use a 5/30 ARM on most of my rental properties.

Each portfolio lender has different terms and loan programs. With my portfolio lender, I can put 20 percent down on as many properties as I can qualify for, and they also offer financing for my fix and flips at 80 percent of the purchase price and, right now, only 5.25 percent interest. I must pay one point on my fix-and-flip loans and do not need an appraisal if the loan amount is less than $100,000. I have a commitment for up to $1,000,000 of loans with them, but each property still has an individual loan against it. Every year, I must renew my commitment and prove I am still in good financial standing.

I found another portfolio lender who charges me 4.5 percent interest and one point. I also do not have to do an appraisal on most of their loans. They will not do as many loans as the other portfolio lender I use, but it is nice to have multiple options. Some portfolio lenders may even finance some of the repairs.

A portfolio lender may want you to have all your accounts and money in their bank. This is usually not a big issue for most people since a portfolio lender will have programs and products that are very competitive with the larger national banks. The better relationship you build with a portfolio lender, the better loans you will get.

How I found a portfolio lender

I found my portfolio lender because I am a real estate agent. I heard other agents mention that my portfolio lender was the best bank for investors. After I ran into problems with my mortgage broker while financing my fifth rental property, I called a portfolio lender to see what they could offer. The portfolio lender had the perfect loans for my investment properties, and it took me about a week to move all my accounts to the new bank so I could easily finance new rentals.

Later, when I bought the business from my father, I asked if they would finance flips. It was very easy getting the financing figured out, and they have been an awesome resource. I found other portfolio lenders by calling or emailing local banks in the area.

How can you find a portfolio lender?

The first way to find a portfolio lender is to ask everyone you know to recommend one. Some people may not know what a portfolio lender is. Ask them if they know a lender that likes to loan to investors. Whom can you ask?

- Real estate agents know many lenders and may be your best source.
- Other lenders may be able to refer you to a portfolio lender once they know they cannot do a loan for you.
- Investors in the area will know portfolio lenders; the trick is meeting them. Real estate investor meetings are a great place to meet investors and get local information.
- Ask your local bank if they are a portfolio lender and what types of investor-lending programs they offer.
- Ask title companies whom local investors use to finance their rental properties.

- Call your city of commerce department and ask if they know who the most investor friendly banks are in town.

Search the internet

Searching the internet is the easiest way to start your search. Simply search for a portfolio lender in your state on any web search engine. I have tried this a couple of times for people in different states, and I always get results. Once you find a bank in your state that mentions portfolio lending, call and ask what type of investor programs they offer.

Cold calling

If none of these options work and you cannot find a portfolio lender, you may have to resort to calling local banks in your area. Call local, not national, banks and see what type of investor loans they offer. If they do not have what you are looking for, ask them to refer you to a bank that might. Keep trying until you have called all the local banks you can find.

What questions should you ask when calling a bank?

Many banks do not advertise that they are portfolio lenders, and many people working at the bank may not even know what a portfolio lender is. If you call a bank who says they are not a portfolio lender, do not give up! Ask to talk to a loan officer and ask specific questions about what type of investor programs they offer. Here are some good questions to ask:

- Do you loan to investors who already have multiple mortgages?
- Do you have a commercial loan department?
- Do you sell your loans or keep them in house?
- Do you allow investors with four or more mortgages to do a cash-out refinance?

- What terms and loan programs do you offer investors? ARM, 15-year fixed, 30-year fixed, balloon?
- What interest rates do you charge? What are the initial costs for your loans?
- What loan-to-value ratios do you offer investors for new purchases and refinancing?
- Do you have loan programs for flippers?
- Do you have a commercial loan department?

Conclusion

This should point you in the right direction. It may take some time and hard work. I had to talk to my lender a couple of times before they saw I was serious and gave me the details on their programs. Just as you must be prepared to talk to a private-money lender, you need to be prepared to talk to a portfolio lender. Provide as much information as possible about your financial position and why they should lend to you.

22. How to Use a Partner to Flip Houses

The biggest problem for most beginning investors is finding the money to flip or the down payment for rentals. In some cases, an investor has a lot of money but no time to find deals, renovate houses, or perform the other tasks needed to invest in real estate. In other cases, an investor may have the knowledge and time to invest but no money. If done right, a partnership can be a mutually beneficial way to invest in real estate.

I don't currently have a business partner, but I used to partner with my father. It would have been really tough for me to flip houses or sell real estate without a partner to help with the financing and mentoring. But in some ways, I think having a partner also held me back and provided a comfort zone that allowed to me to relax more than I should have. Working with a partner can be a great way to get started, but if you don't set things up right, it can be a disaster and can destroy relationships.

How does a fix-and-flip partnership work?

Many people want to flip houses. For many, it seems like a quick way to make a lot of money. Investors who want to start flipping houses approach me all the time. Flipping is a very difficult business to get into, especially if you have no money. It takes patience to find deals; it takes time to make repairs; and it takes expertise and knowledge to learn your market. If it were easy to buy a house with none of your own money, fix it quickly, and sell it a couple of months later for a $30,000 profit, everyone would do it!

Most people who want to flip houses do not take the time needed to learn their market, save money, and research the costs involved. If you want to flip houses but need funding help from a partner, you must bring something to the table. I don't partner with people looking to flip houses because I stay busy enough with my own deals. If I was looking for a partner, here is what I would expect from them in exchange for my funding:

- **Local market knowledge:** I would want any investor to know which neighborhoods have potential, which previous deals would have been good flips, and what the target purchase price and sales price would be.
- **Know the costs**: Many investors underestimate the costs on a flip. You need to account for buying costs, carrying costs, repair costs, and selling costs. I want details, not just that a home meets the 70 percent rule.
- **How will you get the deal**: The hardest part of flipping is finding a profitable deal. Are you using the MLS with a Realtor, direct marketing, or something else?
- **What is my involvement**: Do I have to do any work in the transaction? Do I have to determine value, find contractors, or find the deal?
- **Who will do the work?** Will you make repairs yourself? Will you hire a contractor, and do you already have a contractor? If you do the work yourself, do you have the experience to do it quickly and correctly?
- **What is the timeframe**: Have you planned how long the process will take, and is it realistic? It will probably take longer than three months to flip a house.

In a fix-and-flip partnership, a typical split is 50 percent of the profits for the funder and 50 percent for the person who does all the work. Don't expect your funding partner to find the deal, find the contractor, and handle the sale. What would they need you for?

If you split the money and work portions of the flip, things can get much more difficult. If you decide each partner will pay 50 percent of the costs and do 50 percent of the work, keeping track of hours worked and the finances can be tough. Most people who enter partnerships like this have jobs and try to do the work on the side. One partner ends up doing more work than the other and gets frustrated. Or, one partner puts more money in than the other and gets frustrated. The key is to make sure everything is in writing.

Why does everything need to be in writing?

If you decide to enter a partnership, everything must be in writing. I don't care if your partnership is with your brother and best friend—it should be in writing. There are multiple reasons why:

- **People forget things**: You would think you'd never forget the details of a partnership that involves thousands of dollars, but it happens. I wrote an article about private money a while back and mentioned I pay my sister six percent interest. She read it and was quick to remind me I pay her seven percent! We have everything in writing so there are no mistakes or fallouts from simply forgetting the terms.
- **Partners need defined roles**: If you share the work, how much time will each person put in? One partner may have a family emergency or may have to work overtime. How many hours will each person put in and what are the consequences if they don't pull their weight? One of the biggest problems is one partner thinks he does all the work while the other collects the profit without doing anything.
- **Exit strategies**: With rental properties, you must know what happens if one partner wants to be bought out or must sell. How is market value determined, how

will costs be split, etc.? What happens if you decide not to flip the house because the market changed?

- **Using professional services**: If one partner is a contractor or real estate agent, how will they be paid for their services? Will they get a higher percentage of the profits for their expertise or for saving money on commissions? Will the contractor or agent be paid like they would any other job?
- **Rates, terms payoffs**: If you borrow money from a partner, all the terms of the loan or agreement need to be in writing. Some agreements are a pure profit split, but others might involve private money lending with interest rates, length of the note, etc.
- **Decision making:** Who has the final say on how much money to spend, how to repair a house, what properties to buy etc.? What happens if the partners don't agree? This is another big issue that can cause problems if it's not in writing.

A huge issue with partnerships is when one side either forgets to or does not live up to their agreed upon obligations. If you document each partner's obligations and the ramifications of not following them, the partnership will be much more successful. The partners will have more motivation to work hard, and it will be easier to handle problems when they come up.

Do you need a partner?

Many people ask me how to structure a partnership when they collaborate on rental properties. One question is, "We have the money and knowledge to buy rentals, but we have the opportunity to partner up with another investor. How do we structure it?"

My answer is, "Why do you need a partner? Why bring someone in to share the profits on a deal when you have the money and know how? You will make much more money when you do not have a partner. The purpose of a partner is to provide something that you cannot or do not want to provide. You give up profits to spend less of your own money and use someone's time or their expertise. If you don't need any of those things, don't give up your profits!"

Do you have anything to offer a partner?

I also see many people looking for a partner or a mentor to help them start investing. The problem is they want someone to show them how to buy houses, fix them up, find great deals, and make a ton of money. But the person looking to be taught offers nothing to the investor, except for a willingness to work hard.

I have this partnership proposed to me over and over, and almost every time, there are huge problems on my side of the deal:

1. When I ask the person what they can offer, they say determination, hard work, etc., but they list no specific skills. What can you do better than other people who will help me become more successful or help the deal be more successful? Are you good with computers? Do you have carpentry skills? Are you an expert marketer? Willingness to learn and work hard is not a skill, and it's something everyone says they have. If you want to impress someone, be as specific as possible about how you will help them make more money.

2. Most successful investors do not have time to train someone about the entire investing process. They also may not want to train someone to compete with themselves! Don't be put off if an investor does not want to mentor someone. It is a very involved process that takes time. Paying for knowledge and experience is also an option and shows you are serious. Most people who want free help and have nothing to offer in return

won't even use that help if they get it, and it is a giant waste of time for everyone.

3. Many aspiring investors looking for a mentor want someone to tell them how to do everything. I have had people ask me how I make money flipping houses. I point out articles and direct them toward my book, and they don't want to take the time to read the articles or pay $15 for a book. They want everything done for them without doing any work. If you want to impress a potential partner or mentor, do your research, and learn as much as you possibly can. The more knowledge you have, the better chance you have of impressing someone enough that they'll offer to help you.

If you want to be a partner, you must have something to offer. You need to bring money, expertise, skills, or payment for the opportunity. There are no shortcuts to becoming a successful real estate investor.

Why did I end my real estate partnership with my father?

I partnered with both my father and our real estate team on flips before I bought him out in 2013. The partnership was instrumental to helping me get started after I graduated college in 2001. I could have never flipped houses out of college because I had no money and no way to finance the deal. In return for money and knowledge, I gave up most of my profits. For a while, I was even doing the painting, and on one house, most of the repair work. When I did the work myself, I did not get a higher percentage. I was paid hourly. Flipping with a partner was great in the beginning, but at the end, I was doing almost all the work, and I did not have the final decision on what to buy.

On our real estate team, my father paid the staff, took care of most expenses, and took a big chunk of my commissions. It was nice not having to worry about payroll and everything else, but I also sold most of the houses on the team, and I was giving up a lot of profit. My father also was tired of running the team and managing all the people.

I wanted to take over everything, but I was worried about the time it would take to manage it all and what my father would think. I approached him about it, and my parents said they were waiting for me to take over because they were ready to retire! A good friend was also joining the team, and he could help with the transition. I also had a good relationship with my portfolio lender so that I could finance the flips. I ended up buying out my parents and taking over the entire business. I love having complete control and keeping the profits!

Conclusion

Partnerships can be a great way to get started if you need help. Partnerships can also be a nightmare if you do not have clearly defined roles or everything in writing. Partnerships also evolve, and you may have to be flexible as people's priorities change. My partnership with my father changed over the years until I ended up buying him out. We had everything in writing when we made changes, and that helped things go smoothly.

If you enter a partnership, make sure you take the time to set it up right. If you don't need a partner, it sure is nice having complete control...and keeping all the profits.

Part 5: How to Find a Great Deal to Flip

23. How Do You Buy Real Estate below Market Value?

One of the keys to my investment strategy is to buy houses below market value. This is not easy, and you cannot just call up a real estate agent and ask them to find awesome deals from the MLS. It takes patience, hard work, the ability to act fast, and nerves to buy houses below market. If you learn how to buy correctly, it is a lot of fun, and you will make a lot of money.

I have bought every house I have owned—except for the first one—below market value. I bought my first house in 2002, when I was 22. I bought it for $188,000 and, over seven years, put at least $10,000 of materials into it, along with a lot of sweat equity. In 2009, I managed to sell it for $190,000. Talk about a huge disappointment! I learned that I could not depend on market upswings to make money. I had to buy below market value and force equity into the property.

For my next house, I bought a foreclosure from the Public Trustee. We bought this house for $220,000 by borrowing money from my sister and father-in-law (I had to pay cash at the sale). I refinanced the property and paid them back in full. My wife and I lived in that house for three years, and thanks to an awesome deal and some market appreciation, we sold the house for $350,000. That was a tax-free profit since I lived in the house for at least two years. I used that money for the down payment on our current house.

24. How to Buy Bank-Owned Properties (REOs) below Market Value

REO (Real Estate Owned) properties are those that banks have reclaimed through foreclosure. REO properties are usually listed in the MLS (Multiple Listing Service) by an REO listing agent. I am an REO listing agent myself, and I can tell you that each bank handles their REOs very differently. Some banks repair houses before they list them, and others do not fix anything. Some banks are willing to negotiate prices quite a bit, and others will hardly budge.

REOs are getting harder and harder to find due to the improving housing market. There are still some great deals on REOs, but the deals are usually on houses that need many repairs.

If you find a great deal on an REO, do not be surprised if you find yourself in a highest-and-best situation. Many banks ask for highest-and-best when they receive more than one offer on a property. There is a ton of competition for REO properties right now, and multiple offers are not rare. Highest-and-best situations give every buyer who made an offer a chance to raise his or her offer and hope it is good enough to get the property. In many highest-and-best situations, the winning offer is higher than the actual asking price. I will discuss these situations in more detail later in this chapter, as many sellers now use them.

Many banks prefer a cash offer from an investor, and sometimes they actually prefer an owner-occupant buyer. Sellers like Fannie Mae, Freddie Mac, and Wells Fargo only allow offers from owner-occupant buyers at the beginning of the listing period. This can be frustrating for investors looking for a good deal, but there is no way around their owner-occupant restrictions. It is against the law to pretend to be an owner-occupant when you will not be occupying the property.

You need a real estate agent to buy almost any REO property. Buyers see vacant REO properties and think that if they can just talk to the bank, the bank will sell it to them well below market value. The truth is that banks have strict house-selling guidelines, and they almost never sell them without putting them in the MLS system. Trying to contact the bank to get them to sell it to you is almost always a huge waste of time, unless they are a very small local bank.

Getting a great deal on REOs has become tougher since banks have strict requirements on who can bid and when they will review offers. A lot of my techniques do not work well on bank-owned properties because speed is not always important. However, banks will negotiate much more on properties that have been on the market an extended period of time. If a property has been for sale for 60 days or more, banks will sometimes look at lower offers.

25. How Can You Get a Great Deal on a HUD Home?

HUD homes can be an incredible opportunity for investors. However, some investors are apprehensive about bidding on HUD homes because purchasing one is much different from purchasing a traditional listing or even an REO. HUD also gives priority to owner-occupant buyers over investors. Once you know the HUD system, it becomes very easy to submit bids and buy HUD homes. I happen to be a HUD listing broker, and I know the HUD system very well.

HUD homes are properties that have been repossessed by the bank after going through foreclosure. HUD homes were previously purchased with government insured FHA loans. Many homes that have FHA loans and go through foreclosure are returned to HUD (The Department of Housing and Urban Development). When HUD becomes the owner, they sell the homes through local listing brokers such as myself and list them on www.hudhomestore.com. Hudhomestore.com lists all HUD homes for sale that are not currently under contract. Once a HUD home has an accepted bid, it is taken off Hudhomestore.com, and the status in MLS is changed to "under contract." HUD homes are sold in an online auction format, and all bids must be submitted online by a licensed real estate agent who is registered with HUD.

When can investors bid on HUD homes?

HUD has very strict owner-occupancy restrictions on the houses they sell. HUD has two main classifications for their properties: FHA insurable and uninsurable. On FHA insured HUD homes, only owner-occupants, nonprofits, and government agencies can bid during the first 15 days the home is on the market (typically called the owner-occupant only period). For uninsured homes, the owner-occupancy-only bid

126

period is the first five days. Investors can bid on HUD homes on the sixteenth day on insured properties and on the sixth day on uninsured properties.

When a HUD home goes under contract, HUD stops the daily count for it being on the market. If a HUD home goes under contract on the eleventh day and that contract falls apart, the home goes back on the market 11 days into the bid period. Therefore, some HUD homes have been for sale for 30 days but are still in the owner-occupant period. An investor can see whether a HUD home is insured or uninsured on the Hudhomestore.com website.

If a home is listed as available only to owner-occupants, an investor can see when they can bid by looking at the period deadline. The period deadline will tell you the last day of the current bid period.

HUD typically changes the price on HUD homes every 35 to 50 it's actively on the market. HUD does not have a new owner-occupant bid period when they change the price on a home. Investors can bid the first day after a price change.

What are the penalties if investors bid as owner-occupants on HUD homes?

A HUD home is federal property, which means that any crime committed involving a HUD property is usually considered a felony. HUD is very clear that any investor who bids as an owner-occupant is **subject to two years in federal prison and up to $250,000 in fines**. HUD does prosecute investors who have been caught buying in the owner-occupant period. HUD also may take away the ability for the real estate agent representing the buyer and their office to sell HUD homes. HUD, along with other investors, watches these properties looking for and reporting investors who break the rules.

It is also a felony for investors to make repairs to a HUD home before they buy it or to move anything onto the property before closing.

Why are HUD homes a great way for investors to buy houses below market value?

HUD orders an appraisal on each home before it's listed. That appraisal usually serves as the list price and determines how much HUD will take for the home. For whatever reason, many HUD appraisals come in very low compared to market value. If a HUD home makes it through the owner-occupant bid period, they can be a great opportunity for investors. Uninsured HUD homes (homes that need more than $5,000 in repairs) do not qualify for FHA loans. The more repairs a HUD home needs, the better its chance of making it to the investor bid period. Uninsured homes are much more likely to be bought by investors. I have sold many HUD homes to investors who were able to flip the house or get a great deal on a rental property because they needed a lot of work.

HUD uses different formulas in different areas of the country to determine how much below list price they'll accept. In Colorado, HUD usually does not take less than 90 percent of the list price unless a home becomes an aged asset. HUD considers a home to be an aged asset if it's been actively on the market for more than 60 days. In my market, once a HUD home becomes aged, HUD may accept 80 percent of the list price. If a HUD home is on the market for an extended period, they may take even less. However, discounts are figured on a case-by-case basis, and there is no across-the-board rule. In other parts of the country, I have seen investors buy HUD homes for 80 percent of the list price within the first month. On some aged assets, investors are getting HUD homes at list prices of 50 percent or less.

If HUD receives a bid that is close to the price they will take, they may counter the buyer. It never hurts to submit a low offer to HUD: the worst they will do is not accept your bid. HUD does not blackball investors who submit multiple offers; in fact, HUD encourages all bids to be submitted no matter how low they are. The only exception is when an investor is submitting the same bid every single day. There is no need to resubmit a bid over and over, which may annoy HUD. HUD keeps track of bids and usually notifies buyers of a price change or if they will now consider a bid that was too low in the past. I would still submit new bids if the price changes.

Speed is the key to an investor getting a HUD home. Many investors are waiting for HUD homes to make it to the investor bid period, and most good deals will be bid on the first day investors are eligible.

Investors can also use a trick on uninsured homes to gain an advantage over other investors. HUD opens bids the next business day after the five-day owner-occupant bid period expires. HUD does not open bids first thing in the morning; they usually open them mid-morning or later depending on how busy they are. At the beginning of the sixth day, an uninsured HUD home will be available for investors to bid on, even though HUD may be accepting an owner-occupant bid later in the day. Investors should always try to get their bid into the system on that sixth day because HUD homes tend to fall out of contract more than other properties.

If an owner-occupant cancels their contract, HUD moves on to any acceptably priced backup offers in their system before they put the home back on the market. If the contract is cancelled, an investor who bid on the sixth day could have their bid accepted before any other investors get a chance to bid,

Investors should always have their real estate agent mark "yes to backup position" when bidding on a HUD home. There is no penalty if agents mark "yes to backup position" and buyers
129

later decide they do not want the home. There is also a chance that HUD will accept an investor's low bid if HUD changes the price on the home and the low bid is now in an acceptable range.

How does HUD handle inspection periods with investors?

A very important point to remember is HUD doesn't return earnest money to investors if they cancel their contract. HUD is very clear that they consider investors "savvy," and if an investor cancels due to inspection items, the earnest money is forfeited to HUD. If an investor is using financing and their loan cannot be completed, they may recoup half of their earnest money. I always tell investors to expect to lose their earnest money if they cancel a HUD contract. HUD also does not pay for title insurance or any closing fees that other sellers typically pay.

HUD homes can be a great deal for investors who know how the system works. It can take some time to get used to the system and learn all the HUD dates and procedures. Many investors shy away from HUD because it is different and can be confusing. This creates more opportunity for the investors who are willing to learn the HUD system. My best advice is to find an agent who knows the HUD system very well.

26. How to Buy Short Sales below Market Value

Short sales are another great way for investors to find deals. Short sales are owned by private sellers who are selling the house for less than they owe the bank. To sell the house, the bank must agree to take less money than what they are owed.

Historically, short sales could take anywhere from six months to a year to close because lenders were so slow to make a decision. In the last couple of years, banks have gotten much quicker at making decisions, and some short sales are approved in two weeks or less (some banks still take months). With many short sales, the first party to make an offer will get the house. You must act very quickly when a great short sale deal comes on the market. Remember, even if your offer is accepted, there is no guarantee the bank will approve it. It is wise to wait to perform an inspection and start the loan process until you have written approval from the seller's bank that your offer is accepted.

You must be careful when buying off-market properties as short sales. The banks are very strict about which offers they accept. If a buyer and seller are using a short sale to sell a house but don't disclose all the terms to the bank, it could be considered fraud. A couple of years ago, short-sale fraud was the FBI's most-investigated crime. Most banks require that short sales be listed on the MLS by an agent, the buyer and seller cannot be related, and the properties sell for close to market value. A good real estate agent can help buyers navigate the short sale process.

27. How to Buy Fair-Market Sales below Market Value

Fair-market sales are houses owned by a private seller who has enough equity to sell without having to involve the bank in the decision-making process (short sale). It is harder to find great deals on fair-market sales because sellers are usually not in a huge rush to sell their house below market value. There are some cases where you can find a great deal on these sales.

I have found great deals on properties estate sales. Many times, estates just want to get rid of the house because they have issues or creditors that need to be paid quickly. I have also purchased a house that the seller had recently bought as a foreclosure. It needed a lot of work, and the sellers did not have the money needed to complete the repairs. The market appreciated enough that they could sell.

Investor-owned houses are another example of sales that an investor can purchase below market value. Investor-owned houses are usually rented, and although they may be perfect for a first-time homebuyer, the homebuyer cannot wait three months for the tenants to evacuate. The only choice for the investor is to sell the house to another investor at a discount. There are also investors who try to flip houses but run out of money and must sell before the house is completed.

When you buy houses in rapidly appreciating markets, it also creates opportunity. Some real estate agents may not be keeping up with current prices. I have bought numerous houses where the agent underpriced the property and I was the first to make an offer.

I buy many of my flips and rentals as fair market sales. We will talk about strategies for buying these properties in later sections about making offers.

28. How to get Great Deals from the MLS

Some investors will tell you that it is impossible to find rentals or flips on the MLS (multiple listing service). I buy almost all my flips and rentals from the MLS. Even if you are not an agent, you can still get deals from the MLS, but you must have a great agent (more on that later). Short sales, REOs, fair-market listings, and estate sales can all be bought from the MLS. We have talked about what those properties are, but this section will go into detail on exactly how I buy those houses.

There are many deals on the MLS if you know how to find them, and in my opinion, it is easier to buy from the MLS than from other places. I used to buy many of my fix and flips from trustee sales, but there is so much competition that trustee-sale prices are higher than on the MLS! I would rather buy from the MLS, where I can complete an inspection, see the house, and get a loan.

I still buy REOs and short sales, but more of my purchases have been traditional or estate sales. Prices are rising in many areas of the country, and that creates opportunity for investors. With rising prices, more fair-market sellers can sell their houses.

A fair-market sale is one that is not in an REO or short-sale situation. In the last few years, while prices were lower, many homeowners bought foreclosures and homes in disrepair. Not all homeowners had the money or time to repair the house once they moved in. Some of those homeowners need to sell a house that is in poor condition. A house that needs repairs creates opportunities. The more work a house needs, the bigger discount it takes to sell it. Rental property number five was a fair-market sale. It needed a lot of work and was a great deal. I bought it for $88,000, and two and a half years later, it was worth $170,000. You can find detailed numbers and videos of all my rentals on investfourmore.com.

How can rising house prices create opportunity on the MLS?

With rising prices, real estate agents or sellers sometimes underprice properties. I have bought a couple of underpriced houses recently, and either my offer was accepted right away or I won in a multiple-offer situation. Houses may be underpriced because the real estate agent did not know the true value due to an increasing market or because the seller wanted to sell quickly.

Rental properties nine and ten were underpriced fair-market sales. I purchased rental property nine for $130,000, and with only $3,000 of work, it was worth $180,000. I purchased rental property ten for $99,000, and with a minimal amount of work, it was worth $150,000. If a real estate agent doesn't pay attention to market price increases, doesn't realize a house needs some work, or if the sellers simply want to sell their house quickly, investors may realize a great opportunity.

Some sellers get into trouble and cannot make their payments for various reasons. If the market is stagnant or declining, these houses must be sold as short sales or they become foreclosures. When the market is strong, sellers can sell their homes, but if they must do it quickly, they may be very motivated.

Being a real estate agent gives me a huge advantage when submitting offers quickly. I check the MLS many times per day. Once I see a great deal, I look at the house as soon as possible. If I like the house, I have my assistant write up an offer and send it to me with DocuSign, which allows me to sign the contract electronically on my phone and send it to the seller almost immediately. By being an agent, having an assistant, and using DocuSign, I can send an offer less than an hour after a house is listed. Acting quickly is one of the most important things you can do when buying from the MLS.

Many REO sellers will not accept an offer right away, but many short and fair-market sellers will. Most banks, when selling their REOs, have a five-day period or longer before they will review offers. HUD, and some banks, have owner-occupied periods when a home is first listed where only owner-occupants can make offers. Therefore, short and fair-market sales can sometimes be better deals than REOs.

No matter what you do, it takes longer to submit an offer if you are not an agent. One way to speed things up is to ask your agent to set up property alerts for you. In my MLS, I can set up alerts to send an email as soon as specific properties that meet my given criteria are listed. I set these alerts so I will not miss a great deal on the MLS. I bought my last fix and flip thanks to a property alert that told me a house was back on the market. Investors can use sites such as Zillow and Realtor.com, but their listings are not always updated quickly. Zillow also has many listings on their site that show as being for sale but are actually under contract. The best way to submit offers quickly is to have a great real estate agent, or be one yourself.

Offer the most you can in multiple-offer situations

If you find a great deal, do not be cheap! Do not try to lowball an already great deal. Offer the most you can while still making your desired profit. You also do not want to stretch your limits. It does not make sense to buy a house that will not make you money.

I may try to offer a little less than I want to pay if I think I can get my offer in before any others. If the deal is amazing, I offer full price or sometimes even a bit higher in hopes that the seller will sign my offer before any others come in.

When some sellers (most REOs) get more than one offer, they will ask for highest-and-best. They want every bidder to make their very best offer, and the seller will choose the best offer. In a multiple-offer situation, I do not pay attention to the list price. I offer the most I can that will still make me my desired profit. Sometimes, I offer less than the listing price, and sometimes I offer more. Do not be scared off by a multiple-offer situation!

I constantly hear buyers say they do not want to get in a bidding war. Why not? A bidding war means that a house is priced great and many people want it. Why would other people being interested in a house make you not want to buy it? I think that too many people let their emotions get in the way, and they feel the seller should have just accepted their offer and ignored the others. Do not let your emotions stop you from getting a good deal! It makes no sense to withdraw your offer in a highest-and-best situation.

Make your offer more appealing by using cash or few contingencies

I am an experienced investor, and I am in a great place where I can offer cash on a property if necessary. I also have a great portfolio lender that does not require an appraisal on loans under $100,000. Most sellers want quick and easy closings, so a cash offer is usually the most enticing to them. If you must use financing, use as few contingencies as you can. I can remove the appraisal contingency on most of my financed offers, and I will even remove my inspection contingency in some cases.

On my last three deals, I removed my inspection contingency, and I know that helped get my offer accepted. This is risky for someone who does not know what to look for in a house, but if you are getting a good enough deal and know what to look for, it may be a good strategy. A cash offer with no inspection contingency will often get accepted over a higher offer with financing and inspection contingencies. However, some sellers, such as HUD, only care about the net price to them and do not care if you use cash or a loan.

Use real estate agent mistakes to your advantage on the MLS

I have bought many houses from the MLS that were listed incorrectly. I bought a house from HUBZU where the listing said no basement, when in fact the house had a full, finished basement with two bedrooms and a bath. I recently bought a rental listed as a three bedroom, two-bath house that was actually a five bedroom, two-bath house. You must know your market, pay attention to the listing photos, and confirm the information in the listing. Do not be afraid to look at many houses to find the few that are not listed correctly. The more market knowledge you have and the more experience you gain, the easier it will be to spot the mistakes.

You need to be flexible when buying from the MLS

The buyer cannot occupy some houses until months after the sale due to existing tenants. In these situations, competition is lower because most owner-occupants will not want to buy a home that they cannot move into right away. Many times, the tenants can be difficult when you are trying to show the house, or they may not keep the house clean, which decreases the amount the seller can get. The worse the tenant, the better the deal for the buyer!

How do you know when one seller is more motivated to negotiate than another?

When you flip houses or buy rentals, you must get an awesome deal in order to profit. Ninety-seven percent of the houses on the MLS will not work for flipping because there is not enough profit after all the costs are considered. Some houses listed on the MLS can be awesome deals, but the list price does not indicate how much the seller is willing to take. I do not advocate submitting low offers on every house hoping one seller will accept 50 percent of list price. However, some sellers will take significantly less than asking price if you know what to look for.

- **Aged listings**: Some houses sit on the market for months. Many times, the sellers priced it too high, it was hard to set up a showing on the house, it needed major repairs, or other factors caused it not to sell. Not every aged listing can be bought for much less than asking price, but some can. HUD homes that are on the market more than 60 days can sometimes be bought at a significant discount. Some sellers will not lower their price when their house does not sell, but may take less than asking price. It does not hurt to submit low offers on homes that have been on the market a long time, but look for other signs as well.
- **MLS comments**: Some comments in the MLS descriptions shout: *make a low offer!* If you see the words "as-is," "seller motivated," "quick-close preferred," "cash deal," "no financing," "will not go FHA," "out-of-state owner," "needs work," "needs TLC," or anything else that indicates the house needs work and the seller wants it gone quickly, they may be more willing to negotiate.
- **Fast price changes**: If a house does not sell right away, the seller will usually lower the price. I see house prices

138

lowered around the 30- to 60-day mark in most cases. However, I occasionally see a house pop up on the market, and in only seven or ten days, the price changes. This indicates to me that the seller wants it gone quickly! The bigger the price change, the quicker they want it gone.

- **Back on the market**: Houses go under contract and then come back on the market all the time. However, in some cases, a contract falling apart can indicate a house with major problems, or it can also motivate the seller. When I see a house come back on the market at a decent price, I will ask the agent why it came back on the market. Sometimes the agent will indicate it was buyer financing or a problem with the inspection. In some cases, the agent will indicate the seller wants to get rid of the house because they were expecting it to sell and the contract fell apart. A house returning to the market with a price change indicates a very motivated seller! If a house repeatedly goes under contract and then comes back on the market, the seller may be motivated to get the deal done through a cash offer with no inspection.

How low should you bid?

As I mentioned earlier, if the house is already an awesome deal, do not be afraid to offer list price or higher if the numbers work. Many of my deals were houses that I bought well below list price because I saw some of the situations mentioned above and knew that the sellers were motivated.

I rarely, if ever, submit an extremely low offer. I have never submitted an offer that was 50 percent or less than list price. When I submit a low offer, it is usually about 70 to 80 percent of list price. Offers lower than 70 percent of list price usually offend the seller, and even a 70 percent offer might offend them. I do not submit low offers on every house on the MLS, but I select listings that I think will more likely be negotiable.

When I make my first offer, I do not offer the most I can pay. I leave some room for negotiation because the seller most likely won't accept my low offer. I recently bought a house listed for $109,900. This was a good price, although not for a flip because of the work needed. Seven days after the house was listed, the seller lowered the price to $104,900. I noticed in the comments that the house needed TLC, was dirty because previous tenants had just moved out, and would not qualify for financing. This was music to my ears! I knew the seller was motivated because they would not spend $150 to clean the house. I offered $80,000 with no inspection and a cash closing in 20 days. The seller countered at $85,000, which I happily accepted. Many times, the seller will want to negotiate at least a little so they feel like they got the most money they could out of the house.

What if the seller will not come down low enough to make a deal?

Not every offer I make is accepted. In fact, most houses I make offers on, I do not end up buying. If you want to be a great real estate investor, you cannot be afraid to have your offer rejected or to see someone else get a deal you were hoping to buy. The fastest way an investor can get into trouble is by paying too much for a house. If the seller will not come down to a price that makes sense for you, do not force the issue and pay too much! Even if the seller does not accept your offer, you still may get the house later.

If I make a low offer, I can usually tell how motivated the seller is. If the seller rejects my offer or acts offended by it, I forget about the house and move on. It is not worth my time to negotiate if the seller is not coming close to my price. If the seller comes down significantly from their list price, I know I have a chance of getting something together. Sometimes, we cannot get together on the price or they accept another offer.

In those cases, I am always polite and ask their agent to let me know if anything happens or if the seller is interested in my offer later. Many times, the first offer that was accepted falls apart because it was an owner-occupant who later realized how much work the house needed, or maybe a wholesaler got the house under contract but could not find a buyer. Do not give up if another offer is accepted, and do not burn bridges.

Should you try to negotiate with the seller on inspection items?

When I make offers, I do not ask for an inspection period. I have enough experience to know what major issues to look for and what repairs are needed. If you are a new investor, I would not suggest waiving the inspection. Waiving the inspection period gets me many deals, especially when a house comes back on the market. Many of the houses I am interested in have motivated sellers who want to sell the house quickly. It costs them time and money if they must put the house back on the market due to inspection problems. Every time a house comes back on the market, buyers wonder what is wrong with it, and sellers won't receive the price they want.

If I make an offer without an inspection or financing contingency, the seller knows they will get my earnest money if I do not buy the house. This gives me an advantage, and I have bought many houses at a lower price than other investors were offering because I waived my inspection.

Buyers assume they will be able to use the inspection to ask for a lower price. I do not do this because I feel it is not operating in good faith. While this tactic may work a couple of times, it will also give the buyer a reputation of always asking for a lower price on inspection. Another reason I get so many deals is that agents know me and know I do not play games. If I write a contract for a certain price, I buy the house at the price I say I will. Building a good reputation will give you a better

141

chance of having your offers accepted in the future. If you are only going to buy a few houses, it may make sense to negotiate hard. If you want to be a serious investor, negotiating too hard can hurt you in the long run.

Buying from the MLS is not impossible; it is actually my favorite way to buy houses. I am in Colorado, which has one of the hottest markets in the country. You cannot use the excuse that buying from the MLS does not work in my market. There will always be deals on the MLS if you know how to spot them and can act quickly.

29. How to Get Great Deals below Market from Auctions

Buying a house from a foreclosure auction is another way to get a great deal, but it comes with risk. Auctions tend to have less competition because they have stricter requirements for buyers, and many times you cannot inspect the house or even see the inside of it before buying. I have bought many houses from auctions over the years and made money on most, but I have also lost money on a few.

The fewer people you must compete with, the better chance you have of getting a great deal. Many times, auction companies have strict criteria.

- **Cash purchases:** Many auctions require the buyer to pay cash for houses on which they bid. Foreclosure auctions may require the buyer to have cash the same day they bid or before they bid on a property.
- **No inspections:** Many auctions do not allow buyers to inspect a house before they bid. In some cases, a house may be occupied, and the buyer cannot inspect the interior until they buy. I am currently buying an occupied house, and I have never seen the interior. If the house is occupied, you cannot just kick out the occupant. You must evict them or possibly honor their lease if they have one.
- **Non-refundable earnest money**: When you buy a house, you must submit earnest money to the seller. In a normal sale, if the financing falls through or you find a problem in your inspection, you usually get your earnest money back. With an auction property, if you back out of the contract for any reason, you usually do not get your earnest money back.
- **Short notice:** Some state foreclosure sales give buyers very little time to know what houses will be bid on and

how much the starting bids will be. Other online auctions give buyers much more notice before an auction. In Colorado, we are given the sale list for properties two days before the sale.

- **Clear title**: Many foreclosure auctions do not guarantee clear title. There is no guarantee you are even bidding on the first loan.

These factors make it tough for most buyers to purchase houses from auctions. The majority of homebuyers are owner-occupants who need to get a loan. Most investors also need a loan to buy property, and auctions that require cash eliminate those buyers as well. Many buyers fear auctions because of the possibility of losing earnest money, the lack of inspections, and other issues. That usually leaves experienced investors to battle over the properties. Experienced investors know how much they can pay for houses, can handle the risk, and can still make money. Some online auctions are less risky than foreclosure auctions, which can provide opportunities for less-experienced buyers.

How does the foreclosure auction work in Colorado?

Different types of real estate auctions come with varying degrees of risk. The riskiest are the local foreclosure sales, because they require the quickest payment with the least amount of due diligence available. Every state has different laws regarding foreclosure auctions, which makes it very tough for inexperienced buyers. Make sure you know your local laws before bidding!

A foreclosure auction gives the public a chance to buy houses that are being foreclosed on by the bank or other lien holders. Before the lien holder can take possession of the house through a foreclosure, they must offer it for auction. The bank or lien holder will make a starting bid, which may be what is

144

owed on the loan including late fees and interest. The bank can also start the bidding at less than what is owed.

If no one bids at the foreclosure sale, the house will go back to the bank. However, investors or even owner-occupied bidders can buy houses at the foreclosure sale if they bid more than the banks bid (assuming the bank is not bidding as well, which is possible). I used to buy most of my fix and flips at the foreclosure sale in Colorado, and I even bought a personal residence at the foreclosure sale. We stopped buying at the foreclosure sale for the most part because competition has increased, pushing prices too high. In my area, I can get a better deal on the MLS than I can at the foreclosure sale.

This is how the foreclosure sale works in Colorado:

- The pre-sale list is published every Monday afternoon, which lists the properties and the starting bid.
- The foreclosure sale happens Wednesday morning at 10 a.m. You can call the public trustees office on Wednesday before the sale to see if the properties you are interested in are still going to auction.
- The auction is conducted at 10 a.m., and all bidders must register in person at the public trustee office before the auction. The auction is live and goes very quickly.
- The winning bidders have until noon on Wednesday to come back to the office with a cashier's check for the full amount of the bid. If the winning bidder does not show up, the second highest bidder is notified and given a chance to buy the property at their highest bid.
- There is a short redemption period (8 days) for junior lienholders in Colorado. A junior lienholder can redeem the property by paying off the first bid amount in full, plus interest.

In Colorado, there is no guarantee you are bidding on a first loan or that you will get a clear title. The day before the sale—

Tuesday—we would obtain an O&E (Ownership and Encumbrance report) from the title company, check out the house as much as we could, and decide if it is worth bidding.

What are the foreclosure laws in other states?

The process for buying at the foreclosure sale I outlined is only for Colorado. Other states have much different laws, and each state handles their auctions differently. Here are a few differences you may run into:

- Some states require proof of funds before the auction. This requires bringing cashier's checks for the amount you want to bid.
- Some states give much less notice on which houses will go to the sale and what the starting bids will be. I have heard that in some areas you have only a few hours to research properties before they are sold.
- Some states have an owner redemption period where the previous owner has a certain amount of time to pay off whoever won the bid and get the house back. Some states have redemption periods as long as six months!

Make sure you know exactly how the foreclosure auctions work in your state before you bid. I have seen many new investors check out the auctions for weeks to see how they worked. I have also seen new investors bid on a second loan, not realizing there was a first loan. That investor was still responsible for paying off the first loan!

How did I lose money on houses I bought at the foreclosure sale?

I have made a lot of money from foreclosure-sale houses, but I have also lost money because of the nature of the auction.

On one deal, we had the winning bid on a house at the auction. We had an O&E that showed we were bidding on a first-position note, and we viewed the house before the sale. We looked through the windows, and it appeared to be completely vacant. After winning the bid, we learned the previous owners had filed a lawsuit against the bank, claiming the bank did not foreclose correctly. The lawsuit had not yet been recorded, and we had no way of knowing about it. In the end, the lawsuit was thrown out, but it took the judge a year to look at the case, and we had to hold the property that entire time. After interest and carrying costs, we ended up losing money.

In many instances, I had to buy a house without seeing the interior. There are no open houses or showings when you buy a house at the foreclosure sale. Some investors try to get into houses before the sale, but if caught, they can be charged with trespassing or even breaking and entering.

When buying a house that you cannot view, you must consider how much the repairs could be. I usually buy auction houses for the purposes of flipping, so I knew how much my repair budget could be to make money. I would always assume a house would need new flooring, paint, appliances, fixtures, and at least $5,000 in other repairs depending on the age of the house. Sometimes we got lucky and the houses needed less work, but sometimes they needed more.

I also tried to talk to the occupants before the sale to get as much information as I could. This is not a fun situation to be in. It's uncomfortable trying to talk to someone about buying a house they are losing to foreclosure. Most people are friendly, and they will at least tell you if they rent or if they own. Many times, they have no idea how the process works, and you can build rapport by telling them how it works and explaining the timeline.

Foreclosure auctions versus online REO auctions

There are many types of auctions, and some banks use another auction to sell the house once they have completed the foreclosure. HUBZU, Homesearch.com, Auction.com, WilliamsandWilliams.com, HudsonandMarshall.com, Xome.com, and many more sites have auctions for REO properties that the bank already owns. These auctions have much different terms than the foreclosure sales, and it is much easier to buy from them. Online auctions for REO properties sometimes:

- allow financing.
- allow inspections.
- allow appraisals.
- give title insurance.
- pay a real estate agent commission.

Online auctions have different terms for different properties, and you must be very careful about what you are bidding on.

Buying a house at foreclosure auctions can be scary and very risky. I stopped buying at auctions because prices increased to a point where the risk was no longer worth the reward. The inventory of foreclosures in Colorado has dropped significantly, and I think investors who counted on the foreclosure sale for inventory had to increase the prices they pay because they do not know any other way to buy. I would not rule out buying from the foreclosure sale, but I would also make sure you have multiple ways to get great deals as the market changes.

30. How Can You Get a Great Deal from Real Estate Wholesalers?

I have recently been buying most of my properties from real estate wholesalers. I usually buy from the MLS, but I had a goal last year to find wholesalers so I could diversify my business. It took some time to find good wholesalers in my area (or let them find me). It can be frustrating because there are a lot of people who call themselves wholesalers who never wholesale a house. You must be diligent in your search if you want to find wholesalers who actually have great deals.

What is wholesaling?

Wholesaling involves a real estate investor finding a great deal, getting it under contract, and finding another real estate investor to buy the property. A wholesaler could use a double close or an assignment to transfer the property to the new investor. The wholesaler usually does not do any work to the properties, and they do not use their own money to buy the property.

A double close involves the house being sold to the wholesaler and the wholesaler selling the house the same day to another investor. The wholesaler does not need any money to buy the house because the title company uses the money from the end investor to pay the original seller. Not all title companies will do this, but there are some that cater to investors and will. I have bought most of my wholesale deals using this technique.

An assignment is when the seller signs a contract to sell their property to the wholesaler and the wholesaler then assigns that contract to another investor. The wholesaler will most likely use their own contract and not a state real estate contract with the seller. Not all contracts can be assigned. If you are dealing with REO properties or short sales, it is unlikely you can assign those contracts. Wholesalers make their money by charging more to the end investor than what they agree to pay the seller.

How does it work when you buy a house from a wholesaler?

When a real estate investor buys a house from a wholesaler, it is much different from buying a house from the MLS. The investor does not have much flexibility on how long they have to close or other terms. Many times, the investor must put a non-refundable deposit down, and they get no inspection. The houses are sold as-is, and no repairs will be made. These terms can make it tough to get a loan on a wholesale deal, especially if the lender needs an appraisal. Because of these restrictions, new investors will find buying wholesale deals challenging.

Wholesale properties are not advertised on the MLS because most wholesalers are not real estate agents. They also do not want to pay real estate commissions. The wholesaler will find as many investors as they can who may want to buy their properties and let them know whenever they have a deal. The wholesaler will usually send an email to all their investors listing the price, repairs needed, terms, and what they think the house is worth. I never trust these numbers and always verify everything myself. The wholesaler compiles a list of investors who want to see the property and meets the investors at the house (usually more than one at a time).

Every wholesaler does business a little differently, so how they decide which investor gets the house can vary. In some cases, the first investor who says they want the house for the asking price will get it. Some wholesalers will use online forms to submit a contract, and the highest offer gets the deal. If there are not enough investors who want the deal, the wholesaler may negotiate their fee or try to get the seller to come down in price.

When I look at a property with other investors, I make sure to tell the wholesaler I want the deal as soon as possible. You cannot be timid and wait for the wholesaler to talk to you or finish talking to other investors. If you want it, tell them right away.

Why do most wholesalers never complete a deal?

The tricky part of dealing with wholesalers is they never do a deal. There are a lot of people who call themselves wholesalers because it is the most common type of investing taught. There are a lot of programs that promise big money without using any of your own. A wholesaler sells houses to investors who want a great deal. They pay cash, perform no inspection, and must be very flexible with many of the terms. The investors who buy from wholesalers want a huge discount over what they could buy on the MLS, or it is not worth their trouble. The wholesaler must get an awesome deal that leaves room for them to make money and room for the investor to make money. It takes a lot of time, effort, and marketing to find those deals.

I would estimate that 90 percent of wholesalers never find a deal good enough to sell. Here are some problems I usually see:

- They may find properties they think are deals, but they do not know market values well. They overestimate market value, underestimate the repairs, and don't really have a deal.
- They do not know how much profit an investor needs. Many flippers go by the 70 percent rule, and many wholesale prices do not have that much room for profit.
- They assume the repairs are the only cost and forget about carrying costs, selling costs, etc.

- They do not know how to market or don't have the money to market like they need to.

They will not tell investors they have never done a deal, so when looking for a wholesaler, you must be very careful. You can waste a lot of time with wannabee wholesalers who will never send you a deal. If you find the right wholesaler, they can be an awesome deal source.

How do you find a great wholesaler?

There are many ways to find wholesalers, but they are not all effective. Here are some of the ways I have found wholesalers and ways I have heard others are finding them:

- **Real estate investor meetups:** Most areas of the country have real estate investor meetups, and they can be a great place to network. I have met many wholesalers at meetups and have never seen a deal come from any of them. I am not saying that you cannot find a good wholesaler at a meetup, but that is where many newbies go.
- **Search online:** Many wholesalers have websites set up for investors looking to buy deals. You can search online for wholesalers in your area, but again, it can be hit or miss if they actually have deals.
- **Ask around:** Some of the best ways to find wholesalers is to network with other investors, but they may not be keen on giving you their deal source. Besides investors, ask real estate agents, title companies, and other people in the business. Many wholesalers will email real estate agents to find buyers.
- **Look for wholesaler marketing:** If a wholesaler is marketing, you know they are at least trying to find deals. Instead of looking for wholesalers, look for their marketing. Look for bandit signs, billboards, Craigslist ads, Facebook posts, and call their number. Most

wholesalers market themselves by advertising they will buy houses for cash...fast. Tell them you don't want to sell your house, but you want to be on their buyer's list. If you receive a letter from someone wanting to buy your house, do not throw it away. Call them back and tell them you are a buyer.

I found wholesalers by accident. One of them sent me an email because I am a real estate agent and they wanted to know if I had clients who were interested in buying their deals. Two others found me online through my blog. I spent a lot of time actively looking for wholesalers, and the only ones that worked out found me!

Finding wholesalers is not easy, but they can be a great deal source. I hear from investors who tell me there are no good wholesalers in their area. While most wholesalers may not be very good, almost every market (if it is decently sized) will have wholesalers performing deals. If you are looking to buy in the larger markets, I may even know some awesome wholesalers I can introduce you to.

31. How to Buy Off-Market Properties below Market Value

Many investors buy off-market properties that are not listed on the MLS. Basically, they use the same techniques a wholesaler uses to find properties, but instead of selling the houses to another investor, they keep them. It takes money and time to be able to purchase these types of investment properties. Investors send out direct mail or postcards or advertise with signs that let people know that they buy houses. I am sure you have heard of "We Buy Ugly Houses." They use billboards, newspaper ads, and their giant trucks to advertise to potential sellers.

There are some home owners who want to sell their home but do not want to list it on the MLS. The house could need extensive repairs, the sellers may not want anyone to know they are selling, the sellers may need to sell extremely fast, or other factors may cause a seller to want to sell off the MLS. The difficulty in buying off market properties is finding motivated sellers who do not have their houses listed for sale.

- **Drive for dollars**: Driving for dollars involves looking for vacant houses. When you find a vacant house, you try to contact the homeowners to see if they will sell it to you.
- **Direct mailing:** Direct mailing involves sending postcards and letters to people who may be interested in selling their house.
- **Networking:** There are many people advertising they have off-market properties for sale that came directly from banks. Please be careful, as banks almost never sell individual properties without using the MLS. You can use your network of investors, agents, and other professionals to find off-market properties.

- **Bandit signs:** The easiest way to start marketing to sellers is to display a few bandit signs, which are signs that say you buy houses. Investors like to put these on busy street corners or in neighborhoods in which they want to buy houses. Many cities have made bandit signs illegal, and if your signs disappear, the city could be removing them, or another investor who wants less competition may remove them. I do not use bandit signs because of real estate agent disclosure issues.
- **Websites:** If you can create a website to attract sellers in your area, it can be a great lead source. I am not an internet wizard. Even though I created my blog, https://investfourmore.com/2015/08/24/how-to-buy-off-market-properties-from-motivated-sellers/, I have had a ton of help.
- **Craigslist, for sale by owner:** Some sellers also try to sell their houses on their own. They may list them on Craigslist or put a for-sale-by-owner sign in the yard.

How can you start a direct-marketing campaign?

The most lucrative way to find great off-market deals is to create your own direct-marketing campaigns. Creating a direct-mail campaign is not easy, and there is a reason most investors will never venture into this field or will not stay long enough to be successful. I have my own direct-mail campaigns, and I have purchased and listed houses from direct mail. Since I am a real estate agent, I have a couple of different ways to use direct mail, but I must disclose I am an agent and be very careful when buying houses. I always have a seller sign a disclosure that states I am buying the house below market and I may profit from the purchase. **Check with state laws if you are an agent trying to buy off-market properties**.

Direct mailing is one of the best ways, if not the best way, to find motivated sellers. Direct mail involves sending letters or postcards to people who may be interested in selling their house. There are many different mailings to use and many different segments to send that list to.

The first step in creating a direct-mailing campaign is coming up with a recipient list. I use ListSource.com to come up with absentee owners in my area. I also use a company that gives me a list of inherited properties. We send different postcards to each list and update the lists a few times per year.

Once you have your lists, you should send letters or postcards to the recipients. I have seen varying opinions on whether postcards or letters are better, and it seems to come down to testing. Everyone is in a different market, and different lists consists of different owners. With some owners, a post card works better, and with other owners, a letter may work better. Try out different letters and post cards and see which one gets you calls from the most motivated sellers. Usually you want to say something about quickly buying houses for cash, with no commissions and no needed repairs.

One letter will not get the job done. You may need to send five letters or postcards to the same person before they will respond. You want to make sure you respond right away to any calls. We have a dedicated number set up just for postcard calls so we can call them back whether they leave a message or not.

Setting up a direct-mail campaign takes a lot of work and persistence. Therefore, most investors will not do it or won't be patient enough to see a campaign through.

What do you say to motivated sellers?

The scariest part of any direct-mail campaign is talking to the sellers. Many people will call you and tell you they are very upset that you are sending them mail asking to buy their house. Usually, when you talk to them and pleasantly explain you are buying houses in the neighborhood, they calm down. You will deal with some owners who have nothing better to do than yell and complain. I had one lady threaten to call the police if I did not stop sending her letters, but she refused to tell me her name or address so I could take her off my list.

There will also be many property owners hoping to sell their house wanting full retail value without paying a real estate commission. You will also talk to motivated sellers who want to sell right away and are willing to take a lower price for their house. I talk as much as I can to the sellers to see why they are selling, how much they want for their house, and when they want to sell. Usually, sellers are happy just to talk to anyone who will listen.

Since I am an agent, I like to give sellers a couple of options. I am very honest with them and tell them that, most of the time, they will get more money if they list the house on the MLS. Even knowing they will get more money on the MLS, some sellers don't want to list. Or, their house is in such disrepair that it makes more sense for me to buy it. Otherwise, as an agent, I can list the house for them and make money that way. If you are not an agent, you may be able to sell your leads to a real estate agent, but it is illegal in most states for a real estate agent to pay a referral fee to someone who is not licensed.

When you talk to a seller, you want to highlight the advantages of selling to you:

- No repairs needed
- No commissions
- No closing costs
- Fast closing
- Cash closing
- No showings
- No appraisal

These advantages are for an investor who can pay cash for houses and close very quickly. Some wholesalers will use these terms and assume they can assign a contract to a cash investor who will buy the property. Don't lie to the seller and claim you can buy with cash if you must get a loan. Almost all the successful investors I talk to have a couple of things in common: they know their market like no one else, they are honest, and they follow through on deals if they say they will buy a house.

32. How to Find an Investor-Friendly Real Estate Agent

A real estate agent is the most important person on an investor's team. Real estate agents can play a huge role in getting a deal, losing a deal, valuing a property, and many other factors that can make or lose you money. It can be difficult to find a real estate agent who will return calls and respond quickly enough.

I am an agent, and I think it is a huge advantage for investors to be real estate agents as well. If you do not want to become an agent yourself, it is imperative you find a great agent to help you

There is a lot of information for new investors to process when they start investing in real estate. A great real estate agent can make the process much less painful and make investing much more enjoyable. Finding a great agent is tricky, but you can do it with a few tips.

What is the first thing you should do?

As with almost any professional service, the best way to find someone good is through referrals. The first thing I do when I need help from a professional is ask my friends, family, and co-workers for a recommendation. It is usually best to ask as many people as possible until you start seeing the same name pop up repeatedly. Even if you get a great referral for an agent, you want to make sure the agent knows what they are doing. I have been referred agents that turned out horribly (when I was looking to buy out-of-state).

People become real estate agents for a variety of reasons. Some want a little extra money, some want free time, some think it is a way to get rich quickly, and others want to make a career out of it. You want to find the career agent who cares about their job and business, not the agent looking to get rich quickly.

Answering the phone or returning a call quickly is the first sign of a good agent. The phone call from a potential client is one of the best leads for an agent, yet many agents ignore calls or take days to return calls. If you call a potential real estate agent, they should either answer their phone or call you back within a couple of hours. Getting a quick return call is important because investors need speed to get the good deals. If it takes an agent a day or two to call you back, it could mean the difference between getting an offer accepted and another buyer getting the property.

Sometimes the busiest agents cannot answer their phone or return calls right away. Usually the busiest agents are the best agents, but you must ask yourself if you want an extremely busy agent working for you. Once again, they may be a great agent, but if they have too many clients preventing them from acting quickly, they may not be the right agent for you.

When looking for an investor-friendly agent, make sure they are competent

After you find an agent who answers their phone, you still have a lot of work to do. You must make sure they know what they are doing. Test their knowledge by asking these simple questions about the types of houses you are looking to buy.

1. Have you sold many REO properties?

2. Have you sold HUD homes? Does your office have an NAID number?

3. How do you suggest buyers handle multiple offer situations?

4. How do short sales work?

5. If I were to sell one of my houses, how would you market it?

You should already know the answers to most of these questions, but you want to know if your agent knows. How confident are they when answering these questions? If they are newer and do not know everything, that is okay. They should tell you that they do not know but they will find out. Real estate is a serious business, and there are severe consequences for fraud or mistakes. You do not want your Realtor pretending to know how to do things then getting you in trouble.

Is it smart to work with a new real estate agent?

Some people do not like working with new agents because they are inexperienced. New real estate agents can make up for that inexperience with ambition. Most new agents are motivated and excited about starting a new career. When I started, I was very eager to work with buyers, and I worked very hard for the few clients I had. As I obtained more clients and more business, I could not give each client as much attention. I will be honest and say I am now a horrible agent for investors. I do not have time to show houses, write offers, or check on offers. I hand off leads to other agents on my team who have time. That is another thing a new agent has going for them: they most likely have plenty of time to work for you.

Many investors are very demanding of their real estate agent. They need to act quickly and may make many offers before getting one accepted. If you are an investor who wants to make hundreds of low-ball offers, make sure you motivate your agent. They are only paid when they sell a house, not when you make offers. If they think it is a waste of time to submit low offer after low offer, they are not going to work hard for you. Buy them lunch or dinner and discuss strategies. Show them you care and give them a reason to keep working hard. Even

161

though lunch will not make up for the hours of time they spend, it may be enough to keep them going until you get a deal done and they make some real money.

Is your real estate agent knowledgeable about rental properties?

If you are planning to buy rental properties, it helps if your agent knows the rental market and investment property market. It helps tremendously if they can help you determine rents or at least back up your thinking on potential deals. It gives you that extra push to move forward on deals, and they may see potential problems that you do not see. You still need to know your market and be able to make decisions on deals yourself. Do not rely solely on your real estate agent to determine what a good deal is. If they are not familiar with rentals, that is okay. Many agents do not have a clue about real estate investing; acting fast for you is much more important.

Being ethical is a very important issue for investors or anyone using a real estate agent. Many buyers want an agent who stretches the rules to get them deals. If a buyer or seller knows an agent is being unethical or breaking laws, the buyer or seller is also liable and can be held just as responsible as the agent. Even if the buyer or seller does not know their agent is being unethical, they can still be held responsible.

HUD homes are a great example of how buyers and agents can get in trouble. If an agent helps an investor bid as an owner-occupant, both the agent and investor can face criminal charges. HUD homes are government property, which means any laws that are broken are felonies. Buyers can face up to two years in prison and a fine of $250,000 for breaking HUD rules. Agents can lose the ability for their entire office to sell any HUD homes.

Does your real estate agent have backup when they are not available?

Another very important thing to consider with any agent is whether they have backup. Agents go on vacation, get sick, and have accidents just like everyone else. You want to make sure they have someone who can take over their business if they are unavailable. Many agents work on teams. This is a great way to know you will be taken care of if your agent cannot do it himself or herself. As I have mentioned many times, speed can mean the difference between getting and losing a deal. The last thing you want is for your agent to be out of town for multiple days and be unavailable to show you a house or make an offer.

Finding a great agent can take a lot of work. If you are an owner-occupant who only buys one house every five years, an agent may not be that important. If you are investor looking to buy multiple houses a year, a great agent can make thousands and thousands of dollars of difference. If you choose an agent who you do not think is doing a great job, do not be afraid to fire them. I have had to fire agents because I misjudged their abilities, work ethic, or character.

I have a network of agents across the country through my REO and investing groups. If you need help finding an agent, email me at Mark@investfourmore.com, and I will do my best to refer you to someone.

33. Should You Use Multiple Agents to Find Investment Properties?

Being a real estate agent, I have a definite bias regarding whether an investor should work with one dedicated agent or work with multiple agents. I can also give the agent's perspective on how we work and how an investor can make an agent work best for them.

There are many different scenarios for how agents are paid, but there are no standard commissions or structures. The most common scenario I see in my area involves two real estate agents, one for the buyer and one for the seller. Usually, the seller pays the commissions for both agents. For this example, I will use the HUD commission structure, which is three percent for the buyer side and three percent for the seller side. That can seem like a lot of money for one deal, but agents have many expenses.

Real estate agents must carry a lot of insurance. I carry Errors and Omissions (E&O), general liability, and umbrella insurance policies. Agents must pay for license fees, MLS fees, office expenses, and office space.

Most agents do not keep their entire commission because they pay a percentage to their broker. In turn, the broker pays for staff, advertising, and other expenses. Commission splits can range from 50/50 to 90/10 depending on what the office pays for and the number of transactions the agent closes. Agents also receive no benefits! They pay all their health insurance costs, have no matching 401ks, and have few of the other benefits of a corporate job.

After factoring in these expenses, agents do not make as much as people think. An agent usually only gets paid when they sell a house. Agents may make $5,000 on one sale, but they may have also spent 20 hours with another client who never bought a house and earned nothing for their time.

The reason I am outlining the way agents are paid is to show you that agents want to make sure that the investors they work with are serious and that they are not working for free. This can determine whether an agent sends good deals to you or to someone else.

Using multiple agents to buy investment properties

Many investors like to use multiple agents to find properties. They feel the more agents looking for properties, the better chance they have of getting a good deal. They will talk to agents all over town telling them that they are a serious investor and are looking to make some purchases. This strategy can work in some cases, but it can also backfire.

Most agents can sense when an investor or buyer is working with multiple agents, and a good agent will flat-out ask any buyer if they are working with another agent. Agents are taught in ethics class not to steal other agents' clients. It is drilled into our heads that it is very bad to "step on another agent's toes" by showing houses or writing contracts for a buyer that has already looked at houses with another agent.

Because of this training, most agents will naturally shy away from any buyer that says they have seen houses, are receiving listings from other agents, or do not have one agent but are working with whoever has the best deal. This does not mean agents will not help investors who are working with multiple agents, but they probably will not put a lot of effort into it.

Agents are usually able to show a buyer any houses listed on the MLS, but if they have no connection to a buyer or feel the buyer is not committed to them, they do not have much motivation. They will usually call the investor if their own listing might meet the investor's needs, but that is about it.

Some investors also feel they may be able to get a better deal on a property if they work with the listing agent instead of their own agent. They feel if there is no buyer's agent involved, the listing agent will take a smaller commission and the seller can net the same amount with a lower sales price.

This strategy can work on some houses, but many times agents still charge full commission. The buyer also risks not having proper representation when taking this route. Most states allow the listing agent to either represent both sides or act as a transaction broker. However, if the agent has known the sellers for years and just met you, whose interests will the agent really have in mind?

Using one agent to represent you when buying investment deals

Real estate agents are taught that the best way to do business is to let a buyer choose an agent, and then that agent will work exclusively with the buyer. There are a couple of huge positive motivations for an agent to use this technique.

- Agents know that if the buyer makes a purchase, the buyer will use them, and they will get paid.
- Agents know if the buyer decides to sell a home, the client will use them and they will get paid.

An agent who knows that they have a loyal buyer will work hard to send them new listings, search aged listings, and work other possible deals. They know if they find the right house, they will be rewarded with a commission check. They have much more motivation because they do not worry that the investor will use another agent on houses that they send the buyer.

166

It can work to use multiple agents, but usually the investor making these techniques work is doing the property searches himself. He is not relying on an agent to send him listings or leads. He finds a good deal and then approaches the listing agent to try to make a better deal.

34. Should You Become a Real Estate Agent?

Real estate has provided me with great income and the opportunity to own a business. When I became a real estate agent in 2001, I did not invest in rental properties. I sold houses. When I started investing in rentals, I immediately saw how big of an advantage being an agent was. I saved thousands of dollars in commissions, found better deals, and made more money, all because of my real estate license.

One reason I get such high returns on my rentals is that I save thousands of dollars on each transaction by being an agent. I also do 10 to 15 flips per year and save thousands of dollars on each of those transactions as well. I figure that being a real estate agent has saved me over $70,000 in commissions every year. That does not include the profit I made on deals that I would not have gotten if I were not an agent.

If you plan to buy more than one or two rental properties per year, you may want to think about getting a real estate license. If you do nothing else with your license except buy your own rental properties, it will save you thousands of dollars in commissions per year. On every rental property I buy, I save money because I earn a commission as the buyer's agent. The commission may be 2, 2.5, or 3 percent per deal, but in the end, that adds up to a lot of money. If you buy three houses per year at an average price of $100,000, being an agent can save you $7,500 to $9,000 per year.

If you flip those houses and sell them, you will more than double your savings because you will save a commission when you sell the house as well. On a recent fix and flip I bought for $105,000, I earned a 3 percent commission as the buyer's agent. I repaired the property and sold it for $175,000. When I list the house, I will save another 3 percent commission. On this one deal, I will save $8,400, all because I am an agent.

If you become a real estate agent, you may not save as much money me. I have a large real estate team and pay a flat fee to my broker, which allows me to keep 100 percent of my commissions. If you start as a new agent, you most likely will not keep all your commissions, but it is still a huge advantage.

Advantages of being an investor with a real estate license

Being an agent saves me on commissions, and it allows me to get more deals as well. Here are some other ways that having a license is advantageous:

- As an agent, you get access to the MLS and can do your own searches for properties without relying on an agent to find you the right deal. Having access to the MLS gives investors a huge advantage because they do not have to wait for an agent to send them listings. I search for listings at least five times per day and routinely make offers the same day a house is listed. An agent can also easily pull sold comparable information from the MLS to calculate property values. Calculating accurate values is one of the most important things an investor can do to be successful.

- As an agent, you can fraternize with other agents and people in the real estate world. The more people you know in the business, the more people you can tell that you are looking for property. Sometimes the best deals are those that are brought to you, not the deals you find yourself. Let everyone you know that you are looking for investment properties, and you never know what will come up. I have bought many properties that were never listed on the MLS because of my contacts in the business.

- The IRS has limits on how much money you can deduct on rental properties if real estate is not your primary job.

If real estate is your primary job, then you may be able to deduct many more expenses.

- If you are an agent that does many deals, most agents will know who you are. If you have a good reputation for getting deals done, sticking to your word, and being dependable, other agents will want to work with you on tough deals. Many properties we buy have major issues and are tough to sell. Other agents know me and know I will do my best to get the deal done.

- I already mentioned the commission savings on investment properties, but there is another advantage besides just the savings. If I save $8,000 in commissions on a flip, I can buy that property for $8,000 more than an investor who does not have their real estate license. That savings allows me to pay more money and get more deals than other investors while still making the same profit.

How can you make money as a real estate agent?

I am biased, but I think being a real estate agent is one of the best opportunities out there. There are many, many forms of income in the real estate business. If you are motivated and dedicated to making it in the business, then you can make serious money. I will not go into details in this book (I wrote another book on how to be a successful real estate agent), but here are some of the different areas that can generate income.

Property management: If you want to be a serious investor, you will want a property manager to handle your rental properties at some point. If you start your own property management business, you can manage your properties and others' properties as well. Not only are you saving ten percent of your rent by doing your own management, but you can also make extra cash by managing other investors' properties.

Retail Sales: This is the most common way to earn money as an agent. Retail sales involve listing houses for private sellers and selling houses to buyers. If you are dedicated and treat this as a real job, you can make a lot of money. Many agents make over $100,000 a year, and the very best make much more than that.

Commercial Sales: Commercial real estate takes a lot more experience and knowledge than residential. It is difficult to break into commercial unless you start with a commercial firm who can mentor you. Experienced and successful commercial agents can easily make hundreds of thousands of dollars per year.

REO sales: REO agents list and manage houses for the banks. Agents can make a very lucrative living if they work with the right banks. It can take years to build up your business, and supply is determined by how many foreclosed houses exist. It is a conflict of interest for REO agents to buy their own listings. Being an REO agent is not a huge advantage for your own investing.

Short Sales: Short sales are listed for sale by private sellers who are selling the house for less than they owe the bank. There is a huge market for short sales, and many agents make a great living specializing in this field. It takes a lot of patience and diligence to close a short sale since banks have many requirements and can take months to approve one.

Broker Price Opinions (BPOs): A BPO is a one to three page report used to determine value on properties but is not an appraisal. Licensed agents can complete BPOs for various clients, including banks. They are usually paid between $30 and $80 per order. Some agents make a living only completing BPOs, and for others, it is a great way to supplement income while learning the business.

How can you become a real estate agent?

You must take pre-licensing classes and pass a test in most states to get your license. Most of my team got their license through Real Estate Express, which has a great licensing program in most states. Real Estate Express has some of the cheapest prices I have seen, although I have not researched every real estate school. I have many more articles on InvestFourMore.com about becoming a real estate agent. I also wrote a book for real estate agents: *How to Make it Big in Real Estate*.

There are many ways to make money as an agent. Even if you just want to buy or sell a few of your own listings each year, I believe becoming an agent is well worth it.

Final thoughts on buying below market value

Buying below market value is the key to almost any successful real estate investing strategy. If you want to make money flipping or with rental properties, you will need to buy below market value. While it is tough to buy below market value when starting out, you can still get a deal without waiving your inspection, without paying cash, and without looking at a house hours after it has been listed. However, it will be tougher to get those deals if you cannot act quickly, waive an inspection, or pay cash.

If you are brand new, I would not recommend waiving inspections. It takes a lot of experience to know what repairs are needed and to know how much of a profit margin you need in order to absorb extra costs that may occur. When I buy flips or rentals and waive my inspection, I am assuming that a house will need more work than what can be seen. Houses usually need more repairs than you think they will after you start working on them and uncovering things.

While cash deals are a great enticement to many sellers, some sellers, such as HUD, do not care. HUD does not care if you pay cash or use a loan. All they care about is the net price they are getting on the house. Many times, I get a loan on houses, even though I make my offer in cash. I put a clause in the offer that says I have the cash to pay for the house if needed but still may use financing from a portfolio lender.

Part 6: How to Repair a Fix and Flip

35. How to Determine What to Repair on a Rental Property or Fix and Flip

Often, a great deal involves a house that needs a lot of work. I buy houses that are at least 20 percent below market value. When they need work, I must have a plan to repair them that will bring me the greatest return on my money. I spend a lot of money when I repair properties, and it is very important to choose what I do and do not repair. I have a completely different strategy for repairing investment property depending on whether it is a fix and flip or a rental.

Keeping repair costs as low as possible, while still making homes look great, is very important to my long-term rental strategy...and to my flips.

Repair strategy for my long-term rental properties

With my long-term rentals, I tend to make fewer repairs than I do on flips. I still make the rental property look very nice and ensure it is safe, but I will not perform as many repairs as I would if I were to sell the house. The reason I do not fix as much on a rental property is that renters are not nearly as demanding as buyers. Most renters do not think of a house they rent as their property, and they are not as concerned with the age of the mechanical systems or the finished details. If something breaks, the tenant knows the property owner will fix it, or at least should fix it. I have found renters to be very nonchalant about light fixtures and paint color, where buyers are very particular about these items. In rental property number seven, I left brass fixtures in the house as an experiment to see if it would be hard to rent out (we usually put in nice brushed bronze). It went right away, and the renters did not even seem to notice the fixtures.

Repair strategy on my fix and flips

In a flip, we always replace fixtures and focus on the little extras because buyers want their new house to be perfect. Buyers will not have a landlord to fix anything. They will have to do the repairs themselves or pay someone if something breaks. A buyer will also most likely hire an inspector who will go through the entire house. That inspector will find most problems, and an inspection that finds many problems will often scare off buyers. We try to have as few items mentioned on the inspection as possible. I know many flippers who have an inspection done on their houses after they repair it yet before they list it. This allows them to make the repairs that the inspector finds before listing the house and to advertise it as pre-inspected.

Using different paint techniques for fix and flips versus rental properties

Paint color can make a huge difference in how a house feels. Dark paint can make a house feel small while white paint can make it feel stark and boring. Many people love to paint their rooms a color that shows their style and individuality. The problem is everyone has a different style and personality. It is impossible to please everyone, so a nice neutral color is the best choice. We use beige paint in all our rentals and flips. If the home has white trim, we use a color from Kwal Paint called Sawyer's Fence. For oak trim, we use a color called Millet. Paint colors certainly look different in different houses due to trim and carpet colors. If you are trying new colors, use paint samples on the wall to see how they look before you paint.

We sold a flip recently that had brand new paint throughout the entire house. At the closing, the buyers informed me the first thing they were going to do was repaint almost the entire house. It may seem like a waste to paint over new paint, but the buyers let me know the paint we picked looked good. Those particular buyers liked color, and a lot of it! We could have just as easily had buyers that would have kept the paint we used for five years. We still sold the house by choosing a neutral color. If we had picked trendy colors in multiple rooms, it could have thrown off the feel of the house and scared buyers away.

Other design choices when repairing a fix and flip or rental property

Just like with paint, if you want to sell your house quickly and for a lot of money, other designs should be neutral as well. Carpet color can range from dark to light, but once again, too dark of a color makes a house feel dark and small. If the carpet is too light, people worry about wear and tear and stains. We always put new carpet in or re-finish hardwood floors on all our houses, whether they are flips or long-term holds.

For light fixtures and plumbing fixtures, the "in" style is currently dark. We have installed brushed bronze fixtures in all our properties for a few years. Brushed bronze is bronze covered in black paint. After a bit of use, the black wears off to show the bronze, which I think is very cool. My wife recently told me nickel fixtures may be coming back as the "in" style. I still prefer dark fixtures with light paint because I think it creates a nice contrast. If you want to save a little money, nickel fixtures are not bad either, but I would stay away from brass. Brass fixtures really date a house and can take away from other new features. The cost to replace all fixtures in a house can add up quickly, easily taking anywhere from $700 to

$1,200 in just materials for basic fixtures from a box store. We will usually replace fixtures on all our flips but may keep the current fixtures in our rentals if they are in decent shape.

Updating and upgrading a rental property or fix and flip

When you repair an investment property, the biggest decision can be how much to update and upgrade. Many houses I buy are very dated, and that is why I get a great deal. The most expensive work usually comes from replacing kitchens and bathrooms. I try to avoid replacing kitchens if possible, especially in my rentals. I also like to avoid replacing bathrooms because of the price to replace tubs, sinks, and toilets, not to mention the labor costs. I do make sure all the mechanicals are working well because I do not want a leak destroying all the work I just completed.

On my flips, I tend to replace kitchens more often because I will be getting that money back right away during the sale. On a rental property, a brand-new kitchen might help me charge slightly higher rent, but it will take years to make that investment back. I try my hardest to save the kitchens in my rental properties and keep costs down. It is tough to know when to replace a kitchen on a flip, but kitchens do make a huge difference in the feel of a house. In addition to the layout, there are so many components, cabinets, counters, and appliances which affect the feel. You can replace one or all the components, and it will be enough to sell the house, but it is tough figuring just how far to go.

We always install stainless steel appliances in our kitchens. They are only a little more expensive, and most buyers love them, which helps you sell more quickly. We generally replace the counter tops as well. Usually, the counters are pretty beat up, and you can inexpensively install nice laminate counters that look awesome. Depending on the price of the house, we

177

may install granite counters to spice things up. Nice laminate counters cost $500-$1000, and a granite slab costs $1,500-$2500, depending on the square footage. For houses under $150,000, we usually use laminate counters, and for houses over $150,000, we use granite. Replacing cabinets is trickier because there are so many different types of cabinets in varying condition. Once again, the price of the house will dictate if we try to save cabinets or not. If the cabinets look solid and are in good shape, we may paint them white. I am not a huge fan of white cabinets, but many people love, or at least like, them.

I will try to save cabinets in my rentals and low-range flips. If the cabinets are broken at all, I will usually replace the whole kitchen. We can replace all the cabinets in a basic kitchen for $3,000 or less from a box store. Box store cabinets are not top of the line, but they offer many styles and work great for us. I am partial to maple cabinets as I think oak has too much grain and makes a house look dated. Cherry is nice too but can be too dark. The knotty pine look used to bug me until I bought a house with those cabinets. After a few years, it really grew on me. The problem was it took a few years, and when selling a house, you do not have that much time. I think knotty pine is an acquired taste, and when you repair investment property, you want to appeal to as many people as possible. We always stick to a light- to mid-color stain and basic maple cabinets. You cannot go wrong with white cabinets either as they will appeal to a broad base of buyers.

Additions or large remodel jobs on a fix and flip or rental property

My general rule of thumb is to never put an addition on a house. In my area, land is not valuable enough to call for an addition, and I will almost never get my money back. Remodeling or moving rooms around in an existing structure may make sense in certain circumstances. I am usually not in favor of moving kitchens, baths, or other major components. It is too expensive to make major changes and usually not worth the cost. In my rental properties, I will add a bedroom if it is easy to do because it adds rent and value to the house. Often, I will only need to add a door or a closet to create a bedroom. I may have to move a wall or finish a room in the basement to complete a bedroom, but it is usually worth the cost. Many times, I can turn a four-bedroom house into a five-bedroom house for $1,500 to $2,000. If you already have five bedrooms in a single-family house, it is probably not worth it to add a sixth. I will add bedrooms in both my flips and rentals because of the added value.

The more expensive the house, the more expensive the rehab

You may be noticing a trend with my repairs. The more expensive the house is, the more expensive the repairs. This is an important point to remember when you sell your house. The more expensive the house, the higher the buyers' expectations will be. Buyers will want upgraded appliances, kitchens, baths, and they'll want everything to be perfect. In lower price ranges, you can usually get away with not upgrading houses completely. On our more expensive flips, we usually make less money percentage wise than with our lower priced flips, especially if they need many repairs. High-end repairs and upgrades really add up and eat away at profits.

More-expensive houses are usually larger as well. The larger the house, the more expensive paint, floor coverings, roofs, windows, doors, and everything else will be. You will even need a larger furnace and air conditioning unit.

Landscaping on a fix and flip versus a rental property

Landscaping can be another tricky element, and much of what I do depends on the time of the year. I love completing flips in the winter because I do not have to worry if the yard is dead or not. In the summer, a nice green lawn can really make a house look great. We try to make sure our flips have nice yards and great curb appeal. We will sometimes add mulch or other landscaping material to make the yard look as good as possible. First impressions make a big impact on buyers.

On my rentals, I make sure every house has a sprinkler system on a timer. I set the sprinklers for the tenants, and we do not have to worry about the yard dying. The amount of yard work we do on our rentals varies depending on the time of year and on what the tenants want. We make sure the front yard is nice, but many times tenants do not care about the back yard.

Repairing and replacing mechanicals on an investment property

When we repair an investment property, we always make sure the mechanicals are working properly. Most of our repair costs go into new hot water heaters, furnaces, and air conditioners. On flips, if the units are getting old or show signs of failing, we will replace them. On rentals, we may wait to replace older units, but we will have them inspected to make sure they are safe. It is best not to wait with hot water heaters as they can rust and flood a house very easily. I will try to keep roofs as long as possible on my rentals, but we replace worn roofs on our flips.

Conclusion

Repairing investment properties can take a lot of time and money. You want to make sure you make the right repairs for what you intend to do with the property. I know I did not cover every repair a house needs, but I hope this gives you an idea of what I do to maximize my investment.

36. Should You Use a Contractor to Repair a Fix and Flip or Do the Work Yourself?

I do a lot of flips, and I always use a contractor to repair them. A while back, I decided to repair a fix and flip myself without using a contractor. I thought I would save money on labor by doing the work myself. Doing it myself may have saved me money on the surface. However, after looking at the time I spent, the money it cost, and the amount of frustration involved, it was a huge mistake!

What kind of house did I decide to fix up myself?

When I did the repairs myself, I thought I would save money on labor costs. The problem is I am not a professional contractor, and I had to learn how to repair the house. This particular house was about 60 years old and needed paint, carpet, new floors, new doors, new windows, a new kitchen, wall demolition, and many more minor repairs. I may have been qualified to paint the house, and that was about it. It was a long process!

This house needed a lot of work, and although I had done minor repairs on houses before, I had never done anything of this magnitude. I was sure that doing the work myself would save me thousands of dollars. The problem was it took me six months to finish the job. I had to learn how to do all the work on the fly, and that took me at least three times as long as it would have taken a professional. I may have saved a little money, but not much because it took me so much time to make the repairs.

Why taking a long time to make repairs will cost you money on a flip

When I flip a house, I use financing for most of the purchase price. I also get insurance on the house and pay utilities, taxes, and many other costs. All those costs add up very quickly, making it important to sell a flip as soon as possible. The longer it takes to do repairs, the less profit you will make.

Let us walk through what my daily bank financing costs are while I'm holding a flip. I am fortunate that I can finance 80 percent of my purchase price with a 5.25 percent loan. Based on this financing, following is how much it costs to own a $100,000 house with a $75,000 loan:

Interest:	$10.79 per day
Insurance:	$4.11 per day (more expensive on a flip)
Taxes:	$2.33 per day (my taxes are very low in CO)
Utilities:	$6.25
Total:	**$23.28**

My costs are less than most flippers because I have great financing. If you are using hard money to finance a flip, the cost per day could easily double. On higher-priced properties, costs will be much higher, and if there is an HOA or higher property taxes, those factors will also increase costs.

A 15 percent interest rate is typical for a hard-money loan. If we use an interest rate of 15 percent on our flip example, the financing costs increase to $30.82 per day. However, with hard money, you may be able to finance much more (one advantage to hard money) than other lenders. If the loan amount was $110,000, the financing costs jump to $45.21 per day for a hard-money loan. Now your daily costs are $57.80 to own this flip.

The costs of a fix and flip add up very quickly

The $23.28 per day to own this flip equals about $708 a month, or $1,758 a month with hard money. Owning a flip can be costly, and for someone who must use hard money, it is dangerous to hold a property too long. It takes me about six months to sell a property once I factor in repair time, marketing, getting a contract, and closing.

I would pay $4,248 in carrying costs over six months, while someone using hard money would pay $10,548. Remember, those figures do not include buying and selling costs or repairs.

How much money did it cost me to do the work myself?

It took me at least four months longer to repair this house than it would have taken a contractor. It cost me at least $2,832 in carrying costs to do the work, which is actually less than a contractor would have charged me for labor, but it cost me much more than that.

One of the most important things you can do is sell a fix and flip quickly. Not only does it save on costs, but it also frees your money to buy more houses and complete more flips. If you tie all your money up in one house for eight months, you may miss an incredible deal because you do not have the funds available to buy another flip.

The longer you hold a house, the greater the odds that the market will change. We are in an appreciating market now, but that could change quickly. I like to sell my fix and flips quickly because you never know what the future holds.

I did not save all the labor costs because my time is worth something

I may have saved money by doing the work myself, but how much time did it cost me? My time is worth something. I was an agent when I did the flip, and my business suffered greatly because I spent so much time working on this house. I had the worst year of my career because I had no time to pursue business.

Not only did my real estate career suffer, but my fix and flip business suffered as well. We were only working on this flip. I did not have time to look for new projects because I was busy with this house. Focusing on this house, instead of looking for others, cost me tens of thousands of dollars.

As a beginner, was I able to do good work on this house?

Another factor I hate to think about is the quality of my work. I am not a professional contractor, yet I was doing jobs a pro should do. I was learning and definitely not performing the high-quality work my contractors would. There were some jobs, like taking out a wall and putting in a header, that I had a contractor do because I did not want the house to fall down. And on some jobs I did myself, I did not do as well as a professional would have.

How much money did I lose by doing the work myself?

I hate to think about how much the decision to do the work myself cost me. Not only did it cost me months of my life, but it also frustrated me, cost me business as an agent, and cost me business in terms of how many houses I could flip. It is hard to put a number on the figure, but I estimate this decision cost me at least $25,000, even though I may have saved a couple thousand dollars on the surface. The work was not that great and that may have cost me even more money on the sale.

Conclusion

In some cases, it may be wise to complete the work yourself. If you are a contractor, it may make sense. If you do not have a job and plenty of time to work, it may make sense. Otherwise, you are probably costing yourself a lot of money by trying to do repairs yourself instead of hiring pros who work quickly and do it right.

37. Should You Use Subcontractors or a General Contractor?

You have a couple of options when repairing rental properties, flips, or even your personal residence. You can use a general contractor who will do everything and hire all subcontractors. Or, you can hire subcontractors who will each do specific jobs. When hiring subcontractors, it takes more work from you but can save a lot of money. Using a general contractor can make the process easier but can also cost a lot more. I have used both options, but I like to use subcontractors for as many jobs as I can for multiple reasons.

How does using a general contractor work?

When you use a general contractor to do the entire job, they will handle almost everything. They will calculate the entire scope of work, hire subcontractors, schedule, budget, and plan the entire project. Using general contractors can be very expensive because it takes a lot of time and work to plan everything. The other problem with using general contractors is they can be very slow if they must do all the repairs. Some contractors may be able to handle huge jobs and get them done on time, but others may struggle the more work they must do.

How does using subcontractors work?

When you use subcontractors, you must hire for specific jobs and schedule the work yourself. The benefit of hiring for specific jobs is they can get done more quickly and cheaply than if you use a general contractor. Many times, subcontractors will specialize in just one thing, like:

- Electrical.
- Plumbing.

- Roofing.
- Foundation.
- Sewer.
- Landscaping.
- Flooring.
- HVAC.
- Drywall.
- Kitchen and baths.
- Painting.
- Windows.

Subcontractors can save you money because they specialize in one thing and can do that one thing quickly. A general contractor must use his own crew or hire a crew. While a general-contracting crew can usually do many jobs, they are not as fast or have the expertise of a specialized subcontractor. Many general contractors will also try to do most of the work using their crew, which takes a lot of time.

With subcontractors, I can have multiple jobs done at once, which saves a lot of time. The roof, plumbing, and electrical work can all be done simultaneously. Some of the biggest contracting problems I've had involved giving the entire job to one person. They got overwhelmed, took forever, and the quality was poor.

Please check state laws regarding repairs. Some states have stricter guidelines for who must be licensed and how to use subcontractors.

How do we repair rentals and flips?

I have tried performing repairs many ways. I have used general contractors, subcontractors, hired an employee to run my projects, and even did the work myself. I have had some luck with general contractors, but many times they bite off more than they can chew. They also over promise and under deliver.

I think most contractors will say they can handle everything and may even believe it but are not equipped to handle large remodels on their own. I have had great luck using subcontractors for parts of jobs and contractors for the majority of the work. Here is an example:

Subcontractor jobs:

- Electrical
- Plumbing
- Roof
- Landscaping
- HVAC

Contractor jobs:

- Replace doors
- Replace windows
- Paint
- Kitchen
- Baths
- Fixtures

While the contractor works on his jobs, subcontractors can work on their jobs. In cases like this, I do not use a general contractor because I do not need someone to schedule and hire everyone. I would do the scheduling and hiring, or someone on my team would.

This last year, I hired a full-time employee to handle the hiring, scheduling, and project management on my rehabs. I thought this would be a great way to give myself more time and possibly start a new business in the future (contracting for other people). The first person I hired did not work out well, but now I have a great person in that position. She manages all the subs and contractors. It saves us money and time since we have so many properties being worked on at once. Here are the advantages I have seen with using subcontractors:

- I can get jobs done faster because I will not have to wait on a contractor to have time to complete a big job. I will have a list of subs and can use the ones that can do the work the fastest.
- I can save money because subs are usually cheaper due to the reasons we already discussed (no middleman hiring them).
- I won't be relying on one contractor to get everything done. If a subcontractor messes up, they will only mess up part of the rehab, and other work can still be done. If the contractor messes up, it can screw up the entire project.

I will still use contractors and still look for great new contractors to repair my houses. Maybe someday I will find that magical contractor who is affordable, has a huge crew, and is honest and fast. When doing 20 flips at once, it is tough to find contractors that can handle that much volume without falling behind.

As a beginner, is it smart to use subcontractors?

The more experience you have, the easier it will be to find subcontractors and hire jobs out. If you don't have contacts and must find new subs from scratch, it can be a bit daunting. It might not hurt to try to find a general contractor and then slowly start looking for subs. If you are just starting out, try not to take on huge remodeling projects that require an awesome contractor or multiple subs. As your business matures and you gain more experience, you will meet good subs and contractors. Make sure you keep track of their names and contact information!

38. How to Find a Great Contractor

One of the most important aspects of my investment strategy is hiring a great contractor. Initially, it costs a lot of money to buy an investment property, and it can cost even more to repair it. If you do not have a great contractor, costs can skyrocket due to lengthy timelines and increased repair costs.

What is the easiest way to find a great contractor?

Finding a great contractor is not always easy and can take a lot of trial and error. My advice is to ask your friends, family, and co-workers for references before you try any other resource. When you do get a recommendation, it does not guarantee you will find a great or even a good contractor. Recommendations are usually a better indication of how good a contractor is than any advertising they run. Real estate agents, property managers, or builders may know a great contractor. You will still have to keep on that contractor to make sure they are doing what they promised. One of the easiest ways to let a rehab project get out of control is through little or no contract oversight by the property owner.

A good recommendation does not mean a good contractor

Two years ago, I used a new contractor. At the time, I had many projects going on at once, and my current contractors could not keep up. I received a recommendation from my broker and a couple of other agents in my office. The contractor was a builder and talked the talk, so I let him start work on two projects at once (bad idea). He told me he had a great crew and could handle as much work as I could give him.

He ended up finishing one project on budget, but the second project did not start for two months! I had assumed everything was going well since that was what he had told me, but the property was 40 minutes away, and I had not physically seen the work begin. I was in for a big surprise when I went to visit the property that I thought was near completion and no work had been started! I called the contractor, and he gave me a story about too many jobs and his workers getting sick. He had told me that everything was almost done, so either he had not been monitoring his workers properly or he had lied to me. That job was eventually finished about four months after it was started and three months after it was supposed to be completed. I never used that contractor again.

How can you keep an eye on your contractor?

It is always best to keep an eye on your contractor's work and schedule, whether it is the first time you have used the contractor or the 20th. In my experience, the more communication and oversight you provide, the better job the contractor will do. I have had contractors I have worked with on 20 jobs, but if I do not keep an eye on them, they fall apart. Here are a few things you can do to make sure your contractor does a great job.

- Communicate constantly
- Visit the property often
- Always get a written bid first
- Get a written estimate for when the work will be finished
- Don't prepay for any work that is not done
- Help pick out materials and paint colors

How else can you find a great contractor?

Besides word of mouth, I have found great contractors through multiple methods. I have been looking for new contractors lately because my current contractors are getting more expensive and slower with each job. I did not get any good leads through word of mouth, so I had to use other methods.

Going to box stores that sell supplies is a great way to meet contractors. We use Home Depot, and they have mentioned a few contractors who frequent the store often and have been around for years. You can also find contractors while they're buying supplies, which is a good sign!

Many contractors advertise on Craigslist, but it really is hard to know how great they are until they do some work for you. The nice thing about Craigslist is much of the labor is very cheap. You must be careful with who you hire and the work they do. There are some great workers on Craigslist...and some not so great ones.

There are many contractor advertisements online through Google or Yelp. Again, you must check references thoroughly when using these resources.

I know a couple other companies that offer regional or nationwide contracting services as well. These companies may not work with an investor that only has one small job. However, if you can offer them consistent work in one area, they may be a great choice.

- Vineyard Services offers contracting services in most states across the country. They have been around for years and do property maintenance on many REO properties.
- Asons offers property preservation and construction.
- ZVN Properties offers nationwide property preservation and rehab services.

Conclusion

Finding a great contractor can be the most difficult part of real estate investing, but it may also be the most important part. It is vitally important you take your time when choosing a contractor. Interview multiple contractors and keep a close eye on any contractor you hire.

39. How to Make Sure the Contractor You Hire Will Do a Great Job

Once you find a contractor you want to work with, you must make sure they do the job well. No matter how good the references are or how great the contractor tells you they are, you need to follow these steps to make sure the contractor follows through.

Why do you need to check up on your contractor?

There are great contractors and there are bad contractors. The problem that many people run into is it may be hard to tell the difference between a good and a bad contractor until they start the job. Contractors can get too busy, take on too big of a job, or not keep track of their workers well. Any of these conditions can cause a job to take too long or to be done poorly. Constant communication, written agreements, and checking on a job, are solid ways to make sure your contractor does what he promised.

Always walk through a job site with your contractor

I think it is always a good idea to walk a job with your contractor so they know what needs to be done, even if you have worked with the contractor before. Make sure the contractor is writing things down while you are discussing what needs to be done. I have had a few contractors write nothing down when I discussed exactly what I wanted. When I revisited the work site, they were doing things I had not asked for and weren't doing things I had asked for. Everything needs to be in writing so there is no confusion. I think it is a bad sign if your contractor is not taking notes.

Always get a written bid for any job

You need to have a written bid when you have any work done. A written bid serves multiple purposes that will save you time and money.

- A written bid makes sure both the contractor and the homeowner know exactly what services and repairs are to be done. You do not want any confusion on what was and what was not supposed to be repaired.
- A written bid lists the price that the contractor charges for specific work. You do not want to be surprised with a massive bill for work that you never agreed to. A written bid helps keep the contractor honest.
- A written bid may also include a timeframe for when the work will be completed. Some investors add incentives for getting a job done quickly. The faster the contractor finishes, the more he or she is paid.

A written bid is a contract between the contractor and the homeowner

Most contractors require bids to be signed by both parties. The written bid not only keeps both parties honest, but it also reminds all parties of the scope of work. I have many jobs going at one time, and I tend to forget what we verbally discussed. By having a written bid, there is no confusion about what was supposed to be done or the cost.

Keep in constant contact with your contractor

If you never hear from your contractor, that does not mean things are going great. I had a job I thought was going well because I never heard a thing from the contractor. I assumed he would have told me if there were any problems or delays. It turns out he had never started the job! Call your contractor to get updates on the job, and stop by the job site to see how things are progressing.

Do not be afraid to ask your contractor if they are on schedule and budget. Ask your contractor if there are any changes to the bid or if any more work needs to be done. If there are any changes to the work, make sure the contractor contacts you to approve the changes. Some contractors take it upon themselves to change a job or add work without asking the homeowner.

When you visit the jobsite, do not always tell the contractor you are coming. I had one contractor who would call or text me to come see the jobsite. Whenever I showed up, he had 6 guys working. However, work was not progressing very quickly. I started to visit the site without notice, and there was never more than one guy working. It was clear that, when he knew I was coming, he was boosting the staff to make it look like he was working hard on finishing the job quickly.

Don't pay a contractor for work they have not done

Most contractors will require payment before they start a job, but you should never pay too much without the work being started. I pay my contractors 25 percent up front, 25 percent at the halfway point, and the rest when they finish. The more you pay a contractor up front, the better they will be slow or give up on the job. We also pay for materials, which makes it easier on the contractor. If a contractor insists on being paid a lot of money up front, be wary!

A contractor can place a lien on a house if the homeowner does not pay for completed work. A homeowner has a much harder time tracking down a contractor who takes their money before doing any work. The contractor has a much easier time collecting for unpaid work and should have no problem collecting after a job is complete. If the contractor insists on being paid before starting a job, be very careful or find another contractor.

Do a final walkthrough with the contractor to make sure the work was done right

A contractor should take pride in his or her work and be happy to show you the repairs. I always do a final walkthrough to make sure he or she has done the work correctly. Many times, I ask the contractor to go back and fix minor things or things we did not notice on the initial walkthrough. Do not be afraid to point out work that you think the contractor has not done correctly. If the contractor is hesitant about fixing it correctly, stand your ground. If the contractor refuses to make repairs or do things correctly, you know not to use them again.

Make sure you do your walkthrough and that everything is fixed before you issue the final payment.

Conclusion

When hiring a contractor, it is very important to do your due diligence. Once you hire one, you need to make sure they follow through with what they promised. If you keep in constant contact, get everything in writing, and be clear on the scope of work, you will have much more success.

40. Fix and Flip Case Study Part 1

I love finding properties, deciding what to repair, and selling for a profit. There are many unexpected expenses, legal issues, and, sometimes, selling issues, but overall it has been a great business. I have talked about many concepts and still have many more to discuss. But now I want to share some real-world examples. In this chapter, I discuss the numbers on a fix and flip that I purchased and sold.

You must buy fix and flips below market value to make a profit

The reason I can flip so many houses is I know how to buy property below market value. Buying low-cost properties and being able to estimate the cost of repairs are the most important aspects of fixing and flipping.

The property I will discuss was for sale on the MLS. I find most of the properties I buy on the MLS. We used to buy 90 percent of our flips at foreclosure sales, but the competition has driven prices up at foreclosure sales, and they're now higher than prices on the MLS. I prefer buying properties on the MLS for multiple reasons: I save a commission on the purchase because I am an agent; I can do an inspection on most houses; and I have time to get a loan if I need one.

How did I buy this fix and flip?

The property had been for sale for months with no offers. It was an REO and needed a lot of work. The bank asked $120,000 to begin with and slowly dropped the price to $77,500. Once the price was under $80,000, I was ready to make an offer, but I missed the price drop and someone else got it under contract!

When the price dropped, I was in the middle of taking over the real estate business from my father and not in a great position to buy properties. However, it came back on the market after being under contract a week or so. I had not seen the house in months, but I made an offer right then for $65,000. I drove to the property and noticed the seller had emailed me a counter offer of $76,000. This was through an online bidding system (HUBZU), and I knew there would be other interest at this price. I quickly inspected the house, clicked "accept" on the counter offer, and it was mine!

The location must be right for a fix and flip to be successful

One of the biggest reasons this house did not sell faster was its location. It was in a rural subdivision about five miles outside of a large town. The subdivision has one-quarter-acre lots and dirt roads with no sidewalks. The houses were built very cheaply in the 1950's with only space heaters and no central heat. The houses do not have basements, and there is a railroad track nearby.

The good thing about the neighborhood (depending on how you look at it) is it is outside the city limits. There are no covenants, and people can pretty much store whatever they want on their property (if it is legal). Since this house was vacant, the neighbor decided to store four cars, a trailer, and various other items. I am sure this was a huge deterrent to most buyers. We talked to the neighbor, and he said he would be happy to move everything. Whenever you buy a house in an area with some questionable characteristics, make sure you do your homework to determine value. It is imperative that you use comparable sales from the same neighborhood to determine values. The neighborhood can make a huge difference in how easily you can sell a house.

Don't be afraid of houses that need a lot of work

This house needed a lot of work, and that is another reason it was so cheap. The biggest concern was the ceiling in the living room and kitchen had dropped two to three inches. I had my contractor look at it, and he thought someone took out a wall at some time and forgot to put a header in. Other problems included a kitchen that is 50 years old with ugly knotty cabinets, one space heater for 1,200 square feet, laminate flooring that was bowed and worn, old doors, old bath, some broken windows, and peeling exterior paint.

The house used to be a basic two-bedroom one-bath ranch with an attached one-car garage. At some point, the garage was turned into living space to create a larger living room and an extra bedroom. It is now a three-bedroom one-bath house, and the best part is it has a huge detached garage. The assessor listed the garage as 720 square feet, but it is much bigger. I hadn't measured the house at the time I bought it, but I estimated the dimensions were at least 25 by 40 feet. Based on sold comps in the area, I figured the house would be worth at least $160,000 after repairs.

Repair estimates

Before getting into estimates, I should add that we discovered an added bonus after we bought the house: hardwood floors underneath the laminate. Why people cover hardwood with laminate, I have no idea. Here is what I estimated the repairs would cost:

Repair ceiling:	$2,500
Replace kitchen:	$6,500
Re-finish hardwood:	$1,500
New interior paint:	$2,000
New exterior paint:	$2,500
Replace windows:	$1,500
Install central heating:	$6,000
New fixtures:	$1,000
Refurbish bath:	$1,600
New doors:	$1,000
Miscellaneous:	$2,500
Total:	**$28,600**

I always add money for miscellaneous items I may not have thought of or that come up unexpectedly. There is always going to be a repair that pops up that I did not see or my contractor could not see until he or she starts the work. The total costs on this flip were not too high because this is a basic house and we were not doing anything fancy. Whenever we try to fix up a fancy house, we tend to make less money because it is so much more expensive to repair a home with upgraded materials.

This property did not have many comparable sales available. I did find a couple from the previous year, and there are some active homes for sale in the neighborhood. It is possible to use active comps, but be very careful because there is no guarantee they are priced correctly. I found a modular home very near the subject property that was under contract with a list price of $154,900. Since my house was a stick-built home and has a larger garage than the modular, I was confident I could get at least $160,000 once it is repaired. I put a lot of faith in this active comp, because it was under contract.

What costs do I need to consider

Repair and purchase costs are not the only expenses to consider when running the numbers. There are carrying costs (interest, utilities, insurance, maintenance) and selling costs (commissions, closing costs, recording fees, and more). We make our offers with cash, but I also have an agreement with a local bank. The bank can close these deals in less than two weeks, and I am only required to get an appraisal if the loan is for more than $100,000. This arrangement permits me to buy multiple properties at the same time and lets me use my cash reserve for repairs and down payments instead of the entire purchase price.

Estimated costs on this fix and flip

Origination fee:	$861
Interest:	$2,000
Utilities:	$1,200
Insurance:	$1,000
Maintenance:	$500
Commissions:	$4,800
Title insurance:	$1,000
Closing costs:	$750
Miscellaneous:	$5,000
Total:	**$17,111**

Notice that I added another $5,000 for miscellaneous costs. These costs could come from closing costs the new buyer requests to help pay for their loan, repair or inspection items the buyer requests, or an appraisal issue. Insurance for flips is usually much more expensive than regular homeowners or rental property insurance. Maintenance covers mowing the lawn or snow removal while the house is being repaired and listed. The costs add up very quickly on these houses, and that is why you must get a great deal in order to make money. I can save money because I am an agent. I actually received a commission check for $2,800 on the purchase of this house, which I added to the profits. If you are not an agent, you will have to figure more than the three percent commission that I figured into the selling costs because you will have to hire an agent to sell the house for you as well.

Conclusion

Our total repairs were $28,600 and total selling and carrying costs were $17,111. We bought the house for $76,500 and our total investment was $122,211 after repairs and rehab. That left us with a profit of $37,789 if we sold it for $160,000. When I think about fix-and-flip deals, I want there to be at least $25,000 in profit after I total all the costs, including extra costs for miscellaneous items. Fixing and flipping is not easy, but once you learn how to do it and do it well, it can be a great source of income.

41. Fix and Flip Case Study Part 2

This fix and flip went very well, but it did not go exactly as planned. The house took much longer to repair and sell than I had calculated, and the repairs were much more expensive. There were multiple reasons things did not go as planned. However, I still made almost $50,000.

My estimates on repairs and profits

I bought this house for $76,500, and I estimated it would need about $28,600 in repairs. I usually underestimate repairs, so I always add another 20 percent as a buffer on my expected costs for unknown items. I thought the house would sell for $160,000, leaving me a solid profit after all expenses, without factoring in money I make on commissions.

What were the costs on this fix and flip?

My repair cost estimate was way off on this house for a number of reasons. The total repairs were about $42,000. I had some unexpected costs, and my contractor also cost me money. I ended up selling the house for $175,000. That was more than I had planned, which helped counter the extra repair costs. To be honest, I thought this house would be worth over $170,000 when I bought it, but it was in a unique neighborhood, and value was not easy to determine. I like to use conservative numbers when I am not certain what a house will be worth after repairs.

How much money did I make?

On this flip, I made $43,000, not including commissions I earned as an agent on the purchase and sale. I have a 100 percent split with my broker, so I get to keep all the commissions on my own deals. I made about $2,300 on the purchase and about $4,300 on the sale. My total profit was almost $50,000.

Why were the repairs so much more than I estimated?

This house had a structural problem: a support wall had been removed and the ceiling had dropped three inches. Before I bought the house, my contractor told me fixing the ceiling would not be a big issue, but it was. The contractor had to rebuild the trusses and most of the roof. A bonus of rebuilding the roof was he could vault the living room ceiling, but the additional roof work cost me at least $5,000 more than I had planned.

My contractor also told me the shingles on the roof were fine. It turned out he was wrong and it needed new shingles, which added another $5,000.

My contractor also hired a new worker who was not up to my standards. I am sure he was not working as much as the contractor paid him for, and the contractor passed that cost on to me. Every time I visited the property, the worker was in his truck, on his phone or listening to music. One time, he jumped out quickly and said he just had to take a break to get warm. I went into the house, and it was 75 degrees with the furnace blasting! I never trusted this worker, and I told my contractor this, but he assured me he was great and doing an awesome job. I estimated that the extra time it took this worker to make repairs cost me another $2,500.

I thought we could refinish the hardwood floors, but the hardwood was not complete when we uncovered it. We had to lay carpet, which cost another $2,000 more than I had planned. The heating system was $4,500 instead of $3,000 because they had to run all new ducts and vents. We also ran into some electrical and plumbing issues that we did not foresee.

That totals $15,000 more in repairs than I had counted on, which is a huge number!

The biggest problem with my contractor on this flip

The reason I had so many problems with the repairs on this flip was the contractor was not present. He hired his workers and expected them to do everything right, with no supervision. He was never at the house and did not know what was going on. He told me four times that the repairs were done, but each time I stopped by, the repairs were not done! His worker would tell him that he had done the work when he had not, and the contractor did not even visit the house to verify.

Most of the work that was done was not done well. Kitchen cabinets were not hung straight, and the new ceiling was not taped and textured smoothly. The paint was sloppy, and there were many other issues. I had to have work redone multiple times, and although the contractor said he was not charging me for the extra work, I will never know. All this extra work took a lot of time. The house was not ready to sell until late February, though the contractor started working on it in November. It should not take four months to repair a house unless you are rebuilding it.

Why I no longer use this contractor

I had a long talk with this contractor about the work he was doing, the time it took, and the quality of work. He agreed there were major issues and promised not to use the same worker again, He said he would concentrate on speed and quality on all future projects.

I decided to give him another chance since I had worked with him for years. On the next house, he used the same worker! He took forever to complete repairs, and he hung the cabinets crooked again! I also was not satisfied with the amount of work done for the price I was being charged. I have a couple of new contractors who have done awesome, and I will never use this contractor again.

The selling process

When this house was finally ready to sell, I decided to push my luck a little on the asking price. Since we now had vaulted ceilings and everything was rebuilt, I listed the house for $189,900. I had many showings but no offers. Most of the feedback mentioned the neighborhood as being the deciding factor for buyers not making an offer. After three weeks and no offers, I lowered the price to $177,900, and I received an offer of $175,000 within two days. I accepted the offer right away and on we went to closing...

During the buyer's inspection, they found the roof issues that my contractor had said did not exist. I had a roofer check it out, and he agreed the house needed a new roof. We completed the roof and made some other minor repairs. The buyers were using USDA financing, and I was worried about the appraisal coming in at value since there were so few comps in the neighborhood. The appraisal did come in at value, but the lender said they needed a second appraisal because the selling price was so much higher than what I paid. Thankfully, the second appraisal came in at value as well! USDA loans can take a while to close, and we finally closed on the house on May 23, 2014.

Fixing and flipping is always interesting

I love to flip houses because of the money I can make and because it is always interesting. I ran into many problems on this house, but I had a feeling I would because of the condition and neighborhood. If you find a house that has a $100,000 spread between the purchase price and selling price, there are going to be major issues, or someone else would have bought it at a higher price.

Part 7: How to Sell a Fix and Flip

42. How to Sell a House for the Most Money

Selling a house is one of the most important parts of real estate investing. There are many factors to consider when selling a house: the repairs that are needed, the time of year, and whether or not to use an agent.

What repairs are needed?

The condition of the house is critical to its salability. Seasoned investors and those experienced in real estate can see the potential in houses that need repairs. However, many first-time or move-up buyers have a hard time picturing a house if it needs work or does not show well. During showings, I have hosted as an agent, I learned that some buyers let paint color or furniture persuade them whether to buy a house or not.

The repairs you make are extremely important. The number and type of repairs will vary depending on market conditions and the house price. Usually, the more expensive the house, the more repairs and updates you should to do. The best way to figure out how many upgrades are needed is to look at your competition. View other houses that are for sale in the neighborhood. What types of flooring do they have? Do they have updated cabinets? How nice is the landscaping? And, how quickly are they selling?

Will staging help sell a house?

Staging can mean many things to many people. It can mean spending thousands of dollars to rent furniture for a vacant house, or it can mean cleaning and organizing an occupied house. When we sell a house, we do not stage. We sell many houses, and to be honest, one of the reasons we do not stage is we do not have the time. I know many investors who swear by staging and feel it brings them much more money. I think staging can create a very positive effect if done correctly. You cannot throw a table and two chairs in the living room and call it staged. To stage a house properly, each room needs to have at least the bare minimum of furniture that someone would want. Staging should show potential buyers what the house would feel like if they lived there. Personally, I like how big a house feels when it is completely vacant and has brand new paint and carpet.

I think staging is very important if people are living in a house. People tend to collect furniture and personal items over the years that clutter a house. The key to staging an occupied house is to de-clutter and de-personalize it as much as possible. When buyers look at a house, you want them to look at features, not personal pictures. You want them to picture themselves, not someone else, living there. When de-cluttering, it is best to remove all non-essential furniture and most decorations. You want the house to feel as large as possible, and the fewer items in the house, the larger it feels. When you sell, make sure the furniture is not too big for the rooms. Nothing makes a house feel smaller than a king-size bed in a small bedroom.

How important is the asking price?

When you sell a house, the thing that will attract buyers more than anything else is the price. When buyers and real estate agents search the MLS, they sort out potential properties based on price. I am always looking for low-priced deals that I can profit from, either as a rental or a fix and flip. Many buyers want to live in a specific neighborhood or in a particular area for a certain price. If you price your house higher than all the others in the neighborhood, it can be very difficult to sell. Most buyers have expectations for what certain areas cost, and if a house costs significantly more than that expectation, many buyers may never consider or view the property. You may also run into an appraisal issue, which I will talk about shortly.

Different types of markets will change how you sell. In a seller's market, there is much more flexibility concerning asking price and the repairs that are needed. I will actually price houses a little highly in a seller's market because there is very little competition. In a seller's market, many buyers are looking, but there are only a few houses for sale. Even if I price a house slightly high, buyers will still look at it. They may offer me less than I am asking but still make an offer. In a seller's market, I can sometimes make fewer repairs as well because I do not have five or ten other houses with which to compete.

In a buyer's market, everything changes. I price houses slightly below what I think market value is. I do this because I do not want to be caught chasing a declining market. When chasing a declining market, you may try to lower your price to get buyers, but you cannot lower it enough to catch falling prices. The house then stays on the market three months or more and becomes stigmatized. Whenever a house is on the market for an extended period, buyers automatically think something is wrong with it. Even if the price is great and the house is perfect, buyers will think there must be some reason no one else has bought it.

One of the biggest mistakes I see flippers make during the sale is pricing a house too highly. Even though I price mine a little highly now, it's because we're in a seller's market and I am very experienced. If you are just starting, be conservative and do not get greedy. Price the house where you know it will sell so you can get your money out quickly and buy something else.

How quickly do you need to sell a house?

If you want to sell the house you live in, the time it takes to make repairs or get the house perfect for marketing does not matter as much. The owner-occupant uses and lives in the home while it is being repaired. If you are an investor or have already moved out, you pay carrying costs while the house sits vacant. Most likely, you have a loan that you pay interest on along with utilities, insurance, and opportunity cost. Opportunity cost is the loss of potential profit on a new deal that you could have earned if your money had not been tied up. It can cost $50, $100, or more per day to carry a vacant house with a loan on it. Trying to squeak out a few thousand dollars on a house that is priced too high may instead cost you thousands.

Repairs will also cause delays that lead to additional carrying costs. When deciding whether to make minor or major repairs, make sure you figure the extra carrying costs involved in making those repairs.

Should you use an agent?

Real estate agents are expensive, but they are worth it. I may be biased, but there are only a few special instances where I would try to sell a house without an agent. It will almost always save you money and time. There will be much more on why you should use an agent later.

What is the best time of year to sell?

The time of year can affect how you sell a house. If you have a choice, it may be best to sell during spring or summer.

- **Spring**: Spring may be the best time of the year to sell. In the spring, people are outside enjoying the nice weather and the days are getting longer. Many people must work until five and cannot view houses until after work. During the winter, it is dark after work, making it much more difficult to view properties.

- **Summer**: Summer is a great time to sell. The weather is warm, the days are long, and many people have more free time. Many buyers also want to be settled into their house before school begins and all other fall activities start.
- **Fall**: Fall is a decent time to sell, but it is a risky time as well. Between the start of school, fall activities, and sports, people are very busy. Halloween and Thanksgiving also get in the way of house searches.
- **Winter**: Winter is the toughest time of year to sell. The holidays and cold weather tend to slow down the housing market. I happen to find many great deals in the winter because other buyers are preoccupied with the holidays. The days are very short and do not allow much viewing time.

I am not saying you should never sell a house in the winter or fall, but it is usually easier to sell in the spring or summer. We sell houses all year, and if you do everything else right, you can sell anytime. When I flip houses, I concentrate on buying the houses, repairing them quickly, and selling them. I am not concerned at all about the time of year. If you happen to live in an area with a highly cyclical market, it may be worth it to consider when you will be selling your fix and flip.

There are also some markets where everything I just said means nothing. In Florida, the best time to sell may be in the winter. There are more people in the area and the weather is much more pleasant.

Can appraisals affect the selling price?

We run into appraisal issues all the time, especially in an appreciating market. Appraisers must use sold comps when they determine value. In an appreciating market, it can be tough to find enough sold comps to justify rising prices. When you are deciding how many repairs to do, look at the sold comps in the neighborhood and make sure the sold comps support a higher value. If your house is going to be nicer and more expensive than everything else in the neighborhood, you may run into an appraisal issue.

If a house does not appraise for the contract price, buyers must base their loan value on the appraisal value. Many times, buyers do not have extra cash, and the only solution to a low appraisal is to find a new buyer or lower the price. If an FHA appraisal has been done, the appraisal stays with the house for four months, and any new FHA buyers must use that appraisal.

I often run into appraisal issues on my flips because I repair them and they sell at the top of the market. The more expensive a house compared to other houses in the neighborhood, the more likely it is that you will have an appraisal issue. If you are planning to renovate a house to try to get the highest price you can, make sure you are not overpricing it for the neighborhood. Not only will it be hard to get buyers to view it, but it also may not appraise for your contract price.

How does the 90-day flip rule affect the selling process?

There used to be a 90-day flip rule on FHA loans for buyers. The rule would not allow lenders to loan on properties that had sold within the last 90 days. Even though that rule was suspended, many lenders still abide by it. Some lenders allow a second appraisal within 90 days of the sale to verify value; some make everyone wait 90 days; and others do not pay attention to the rule at all. Foreclosures that a bank repurchases are exempt from this rule. If you are going to flip a house and plan to sell it within 90 days of the purchase date, be aware that you may run into a problem with the 90-day flip rule.

Conclusion

There is a lot to think about when selling a house. I have sold houses for over 15 years, and I am still learning! If you want to simplify the process, hire a great agent. Otherwise, pay attention to how the house looks, the repairs you make, your asking price, and the time of year. The only time we might try to sell a house by owner is when repairs are in progress and the house is not yet ready for market.

When we price a house correctly, we tend to get an offer around the third week it's on the market. I have no idea why it ends up being three weeks, but that seems to be the sweet spot. If we price it too low, we get multiple offers in the first week. If we price it too high, we get no offers in the first month. If we do not get any offers in the first month, we lower the price about five percent right away. We do not want our houses sitting stagnant on the market.

Of course, this timing assumes a stable market, if there is a shortage of listings, you may get offers right away when priced correctly. If there is an abundance of listings, it could take months to get a good offer. When flipping, you do not want to wait months for a great offer. In a buyer's market, we price below what we think the house will sell for to move it quickly.

43. How Much Does It Cost to Sell a House?

There are many costs involved in selling a house, and knowing those costs up front will make the experience much more enjoyable. You will most likely have to pay a real estate agent, title insurance, recording fees, closing fees, and possibly much more.

I am a real estate agent and investor in Colorado. I will base this section on the costs for selling in Colorado. Title insurance, closing fees, and other costs may vary by state.

How much does it cost?

Costs can vary greatly based on real estate commissions, closing fees, closing costs, title insurance, and more. A rough estimate for the selling costs with a real estate agent is 7 to 10 percent of the selling price. This figure can be quite shocking to many sellers, but if you want to get top dollar for your house, it costs money.

By far the biggest cost is that you'll to pay a real estate agent. There is no set commission, but HUD pays a six-percent commission, three percent to the selling agent and three percent to the listing agent. I will use HUD's commission structure as an example throughout this section. However, you can always try negotiating with your real estate agent for a lower commission.

If you do not use an agent, you could underprice or over price the house, which could easily cost you the amount an agent charges...or more. An agent also knows the contract and selling processes in your state. Trying to determine pricing, contracts, marketing, showings, negotiations, inspections, and more on your own could be a nightmare. An agent can help with all of this and make the process easier, while at the same time getting you the best price for your house.

Title insurance is usually paid by the seller

In most states, it is customary for the seller to pay for title insurance. Title insurance is a guarantee to the buyer that a house has a clear title. Title insurance guarantees that all loans are paid off and that all liens, judgments, and title defects are taken care of. It is always smart to get title insurance when you buy a house. In Colorado, title insurance costs between $600 and $1,200 depending on the price of the house. This cost can vary by state, as laws regarding title insurance are different in each state.

The seller must pay closing fees, recording fees, and more

Many other fees are involved when you sell. The closing company will charge a fee to handle the closing, which can range from $200 to $800 (usually on the lower end). In some states, you must use an attorney to close. In Colorado, the buyer and seller typically split the closing fee, but that can be negotiated as well.

There are also recording fees for the deed, recording fees for any mortgages that muse be released, wiring fees for loan payoffs, and fees for payoff figures, which many banks charge for. These fees can range from $50 to $500 depending on the loan amount and payoffs.

Taxes and utilities may also factor into the costs

In most cases, when you sell, you pay the taxes and utilities up to the day you close. In Colorado, we have property taxes but usually no transfer taxes or local taxes. Even if your mortgage company pays your property taxes through an escrow account, you could still owe taxes at closing. These taxes must be paid at closing before the house is sold. If the escrow account holds extra money after closing, your mortgage company will return it to you.

The same can happen with water bills in my area. The water account balance must be brought to zero before closing. The title company will typically escrow a small amount for the water bill so they can pay the final bill after closing. Any unused funds are returned to the seller.

Taxes and the water escrow can range greatly depending on the cost of the house. Colorado property taxes are low. In my county, they are approximately .05 percent of the sale price. A water escrow may be $100.

HOA costs can be a huge surprise to sellers

When you live in a neighborhood with an HOA, you usually pay a monthly fee. There are also many costs and different payments structures besides the monthly fee. I just sold a house for owners who had an HOA but no monthly payments. The HOA charged a fee of .05 percent of the selling price of every house in the neighborhood, which the buyer and seller split. The sellers were not aware of this policy and were quite surprised at closing.

Most HOAs do not work this way, but many do charge transfer fees or fees for a status letter. These fees can be $20, $150 or more. The purchase contract will determine who pays these fees. The fees could be split, paid by the seller, or paid by the buyer.

What are the total direct costs in selling a house?

Costs discussed up to this point are direct costs. On a $200,000 house, the costs may be as follows:

Real estate agent commissions:	$12,000
Title insurance:	$1,000
HOA transfer fees:	$150
Recording fees, payoff fees:	$150
Water escrow:	$100
Prorated taxes:	$750
Closing fee:	$200
Total:	**$14,350**

The payoff on your mortgage may surprise you at closing

The mortgage payoff on a house you are selling surprises many people when they see how much it is. The payoff on a mortgage is figured to the day of the sale just the same as the taxes are. When you receive your mortgage statement, the principal amount listed was calculated after you had just made a payment on the loan. Every day after the bank calculates the principal amount, the interest increases. A $180,000 loan balance at five percent interest will accrue about $25 per day in interest. If you decide not to pay your last mortgage payment because you are closing on the fifth of the month, there could be 30 days of interest that accrues before you sell the house and pay off the loan. That adds up to $750 dollars and can be a shock to sellers who expect their payoff to be the same as their last mortgage statement principal balance.

Closing costs the buyer may ask for when selling a house

In some instances, to get a loan, buyers may need the seller to pay closing costs for them. Closing costs can range from two to four percent of the loan, and many times, buyers do not have the cash to pay these costs. It is very common for the seller to pay three percent of the closing costs for the buyer. In some cases, the price of the house is increased to make up for the closing costs. Sellers should be aware that many buyers with owner-occupied financing may ask for closing costs, which will decrease the sellers' bottom line.

Conclusion

It takes a lot of money to sell a house, but remember, the seller had to pay those costs as well when they sold it to you. When you add real estate commissions, closing costs, fees, and repair funds, the costs can be significant. If you are planning to use the proceeds from the sale to buy a new house, make sure you figure the correct amounts and are not shocked when you get your figures at closing!

44. Why You Should Always Use a Real Estate Agent to Sell a House

Real estate agents are expensive, and many sellers think selling a house themselves is a great way to save money. Sellers may save a commission by selling a house themselves, but there is a good chance that not using an agent will actually cost them more money than the commission they saved. People claim to have sold their house in one day and saved thousands by selling it themselves. They probably left a lot of money on the table if they sold it in one day, and a great real estate agent would have more than made up for the commission they charge by getting a higher price.

Real estate agents are marketing experts, are educated on the sales process, and know how to value a house. You do not pay them just for the time they spend selling your house. There are many reasons real estate agents charge a lot, but the biggest benefit to using a real estate agent is they will value your property correctly and get you the most money.

You may not save as much as you think when you sell a house yourself

When you try to sell a house yourself, it may seem that you can save an entire commission. However, most buyers work with real estate agents when they are looking for a house. If you are not going to pay the buyer's real estate agent a commission, you eliminate most of the buyers in your market. Eliminating most buyers will definitely decrease your selling price and cost you money. If you do agree to pay a cooperating broker, you are only saving half the commission. On top of only saving half the commission, the buyer is represented by a real estate agent and you are not. Who will have the upper hand in negotiations and the selling process? Who will know what costs are typical for the buyer to pay and what is typical for the seller to pay?

The buyer's agent will have the best interest of the buyer in mind, not yours.

Why is it so important to value a house correctly?

If you underprice or overprice a house, it can cost you thousands of dollars. The best opportunity to sell a house is when it first comes on the market, especially in a seller's market like the current one. There are buyers waiting for the perfect house, and it is vital that a house is priced accurately from the beginning.

How will underpricing a house cost the seller money?

We already talked about overpricing a house, but underpricing can cost just as much money. When you underprice a house, you will most likely sell it very quickly, but you will sell it for less money than it is worth. It is true that underpricing a house can stir up a lot of activity and produce many offers. In a multiple-offer situation, it is possible to get a contract above your asking price. The problem with a low asking price is it attracts buyers like me who want a great deal.

Multiple-offer situations will actually scare away some buyers who do not want to get into a bidding war and will not put an offer on a house that has multiple offers. If you underprice a house and get an offer above asking price, you could have received an even higher offer had you priced the house correctly. Most buyers will base their offer on the list price, not on what the house is actually worth. I hear buyers constantly saying they offered $10,000 over asking price and still did not get the house! They base their offer on the list price assuming the seller is asking fair market value; they don't base their offer on what the house may actually be worth. Another downside to an offer well above asking price is it may give an appraiser a reason to come in at a low value. If an appraisal comes in low, it could cost the seller even more money! By pricing the house correctly to begin with, you will usually sell it for the most money.

Why is valuing a house difficult without a real estate agent?

Valuing a property is the most important aspect of selling a house. It is very difficult to do without a lot of experience and without MLS access. Without MLS access, it is very hard to get information about recently sold properties. Recently sold properties are the most important piece of information needed to value a house. People have access to active listings through websites like Zillow, but only licensed agents have access to the MLS.

Active listings are houses that are on the market, not houses that have already sold. Active listings can give you an idea of house values, but you have no way of knowing if houses are overpriced or for what price they will actually sell. Every house is different. Every house has different features and is in a different location. Real estate agents are experts at determining value based on these characteristics. It can take years to understand local markets, which can change extremely rapidly. It is very difficult and takes a lot of time for an agent to determine value correctly. It is even more difficult for a non agent.

A real estate agent knows how to deal with a low appraisal

If you end up with a buyer who is getting a loan, they will most likely need an appraisal. If the appraisal comes in low, there is a good chance the buyer will need the price of the house to be lowered. With rising house prices, we see appraisals come in low all the time, and there is a way to deal with appraisers. A real estate agent knows how to be proactive to help the appraiser and knows how to challenge an appraisal if it comes in too low.

A real estate agent knows how to market a house

There is a definite art to marketing a house correctly. You cannot just stick a house on the MLS and wait for offers to come in unless you underprice it. A real estate agent knows how to take the best pictures, create virtual tours, create the best brochures, the best websites to use, which magazines and newspapers to advertise in, and much more.

Why a seller should not use a low-fee service to enter a house on the MLS?

Many companies offer low-fee MLS services where you pay a couple hundred dollars and get your house entered on the MLS. There are many problems with using this type of service.

- The service may never see your house and may enter incorrect information without pictures
- The seller must still take calls and set up showings with many of these services
- You will have to pay the buyer's agent if you enter the house on the MLS. Once you have paid the MLS listing company and buyer's agent, are you really saving much money?
- You still have all the disadvantages of not having an agent represent you and having the buyer represented: You'll get no help with contracts, negotiations, inspections, appraisals, etc.
- These services are not legal in all states.

A real estate agent knows how to handle state contracts

In Colorado, the state contract is 17 pages long with four addendums and disclosures that need to be completed. A real estate agent knows exactly what to look for in a state contract, what is customary for the seller to pay, and what is customary for the buyer to pay. In Colorado, it is customary for the seller to pay for title insurance and for the buyer and seller to split many other costs. The buyer typically pays many costs. If you do not have an agent to guide you through what is normal for a seller to pay and what is not, you could easily end up paying more than you should.

A real estate agent knows title companies, lenders, and other agents

A real estate agent knows the market and they know people in the business. They can help a seller find a title company with the lowest fees and best service. They can help the seller find the best contractor if repairs are needed before the listing or after an inspection. A real estate agent also may have buyers waiting for a house just like yours! These costs can easily be more than the real estate commission the seller saved.

Conclusion

It is usually better to use a real estate agent to sell a house. A real estate agent will make you more money, even though they charge a commission. I know many investors who have their real estate license, and they still use another real estate agent to sell their house. Those investors know that another agent has the market expertise and the time needed to sell the house. Before you try to sell a house on your own, consider if it is worth the time it will take to understand the process and if it will actually save you any money.

45. How to Make More Money Fixing and Flipping Houses

Fixing and flipping can offer great primary income or extra money as a side job. It has taken me many years to build a fix-and-flip business that can handle a lot of inventory. One of the reasons I can to handle so many flips is that I use a lot of my own money to buy and repair the properties. Using my own money, with a mix of bank financing and private money, increases my returns and lets me make even more money. The easiest way to increase returns is to buy more fix and flips, which sometimes means you'll need to invest more of your own money into the property.

Is it smart to use other people's money?

One of the great components of investing in both flips and rentals is the ability to use other people's money to finance properties.

The more financing leverage you use, the more properties you can buy. However, the more financing you use, the more expensive it is. I use private money or my own money to make the down payment and fund all repairs. The bank money I use for flipping is very cheap, but I also must use a lot of my own money with this setup.

Why I do not finance a higher percentage of my fix and flips

One option I have to finance a higher percentage of my fix and flips is hard money. The problem with hard money is the interest rate is 10 to 18 percent and you must pay two to five points in origination fees. Hard money may let you finance most of the purchase price and repairs, but the increased cost will add up to thousands and thousands of dollars.

Not only is the interest rate higher with hard money, but if I borrow more money, I am also paying that higher percentage interest rate on a higher balance. I also pay interest on my entire loan from the very beginning, even if I have not received all the money for repairs!

Partnering with an investor

For years, I did fix and flips with my father, and we split the profits. The advantage was I did not have to put much of my own money into the business. The drawback was I had to split profits and did not have full decision-making ability. I wanted to buy many properties that my father did not.

A partner can be a great asset and can offer money and expertise. However, a partner will greatly reduce profits and possibly cause problems when there are disagreements. When I built my business enough to take over the flips, I gained control of what is purchased and became able to keep all the profits.

How do you make more money on fix and flips?

Putting the profits you make from flipping back into the business is one way to flip more houses. To use more of your own money, you must save it and keep it in the business. I like to think of it as a bankroll. Poker players must have a bankroll to enter tournaments and play cash games or they cannot make any money. The best poker players have hundreds of thousands of dollars to pay for both tournaments and cash games and the same goes for flipping. You are going to have to use your own money at some point if you want to make a lot of money.

By using your own money, you can avoid using a partner, save a ton on financing costs, and have full decision-making power.

With your own money, you can avoid using hard money and save on the interest rate. The more money you save, the more likely it is that a bank will help finance your flips, just as my bank does. The more money you save, the more flips you can do at one time. It is a fantastic cycle if you can get it started. When you start flipping a lot of houses, it is also much easier to attract private money, which can allow you to buy even more houses.

How do you save money to invest in fix and flips?

When you successfully flip a house, keep the profits from the flip and invest them in the business. You will have to pay taxes on those profits, so you cannot keep it all invested, but you can keep most of it.

Many people start fixing and flipping to make extra money on the side. When you make money on a flip, do not spend it. Keep it in the business! The more money you save, the more you will make on each deal. It will become a snowball effect, and soon you will have a sizable bankroll. This is how I went from flipping a couple of houses at once to 20 at once!

How much money can you save by using your own money?

Here is an example of how much I would make versus someone who must use hard money.

I'll assume financing costs on a $100,000 purchase price with $25,000 in repairs while holding the property for six months:

With Bank Financing:

Interest on $75,000 loan: $1,968
Origination fee: $1,125
Total: **$3,093**

With Hard Money:

Interest on $125,000 loan: $9,375
Origination fee: $5,000
Total: **$14,375**

If I use my own money, I would save over $11,000 dollars more than someone who uses hard money. The downside is I must have $50,000 to invest into the property. I can use private money to fund part of that $50,000, which I can get at seven percent (many times private lenders will want much more than seven percent). Seven percent interest on $50,000 for six months is $1,750, a little less than the $11,282 the hard-money loan would cost you.

If you have an awesome private-money source that will lend you hundreds of thousands of dollars at reasonable rates, you may not need your own money. These sources are hard to find and can disappear at any time. Attracting these sources is much easier when you have skin in the game.

Conclusion

It is not easy to do, but using your own money to finance part of your flips will make a huge difference in the profit on each property. Using your own money also has many other advantages. If you have your own money, banks will be more likely to finance you, and it will be easier to find private money. If you have your own money invested in a deal, it is much more likely that you will see it through to completion and not give up. Many hard-money lenders will not finance all your purchase price and repairs, so you may need your own money with them as well. With your own money, you can avoid having partners, giving up 50 percent of the profits, and not having complete decision-making ability. Having your own bankroll will allow you to buy multiple properties at one time. Overall, using your own money to fund part of the flip business will make you a lot more money in the end.

From the very beginning of your flipping journey, you should be thinking ahead to how you can scale the business. Saving as much of the profits as you can is a great way to grow faster. Looking for private money and good, local banks from the start is a great way to grow faster. Hard-money lenders can be a decent source of money, but they are expensive! The more diverse means you have for funding deals the better off you will be. If you do not want to ask people for money right away, make a list of possible lenders who you can ask once you have done a few deals.

46. Bonus Chapter: How I Bought My Last 20 Houses

I hope you have enjoyed all the information I have provided. It is a fun and wild ride. I am constantly changing and improving how I do things in order to flip more houses. I know one of the biggest challenges for any investor is finding the deal.

I thought it would be fun to give a quick rundown on how I bought my last 20 houses. This is in order from the most recent purchase. You can also see all the flips I am currently working on my blog at https://investfourmore.com/flips/.

1. I bought this house from an off-market seller who called my real estate team. The sellers' parents passed away, and they wanted it sold fast. They did not want to list it, and I bought it for $140,000. After the $35,00 in needed repairs, it should be worth $225,000.

2. I bought this house from the MLS. It was listed for $158,000, but I bought it for $125,000. I emailed the agent asking if the sellers would entertain a low offer, and she said they thought they would as it was an estate sale. I offered $120,000, and they countered at $130,000. I countered back at $125,000, and they accepted. The house needs about $40,000 in work and is worth $210,000 or more after repairs.

3. I bought this house from the MLS as a short sale. Multiple contracts fell through because people were tired of waiting for the bank. It was listed for $152,000, and my $145,000 offer was accepted. It needs $35,000 in work and should be worth $225,000 when repaired.

4. I bought this house from a wholesaler. It was a manufactured house, and they wanted $98,000. I offered $92,000, and they accepted since there was almost no other interest in the home. It will take about $20,000 in repairs and will be worth $170,000.

5. I bought this house from a wholesaler for $142,000. I am not doing a full rehab, just the roof, paint, and carpet. It will take $20,000 to repair it and will be worth $215,000.

6. This house was bought from a wholesaler for $173,000. It needs a lot of work and is located in the country on half an acre. I am buying part of the neighbor's land to make it a full acre. The house should be worth over $300,000 when it is done but will take $70,000 in repairs.

7. This house is also located in the country on 5 acres, and I bought it from a wholesaler. I paid $235,000, and it will be worth $350,000 once the $35,000 in repairs are complete.

8. This was another house I bought from a wholesaler. I paid $197,000, and we just listed it for $289,900 after making $20,000 in repairs.

9. This house was a wholesale deal that I bought for $100,000. It needs about $35,000 in work and should be worth $180,000.

10. I bought this house from the MLS for $183,000. We are spending $40,000 on the repairs (way over budget) and will list it for $279,900.

11. I bought this house from a wholesaler for $85,000. It needs about $45,000 in work and will be worth close to $200,000.

12. I bought this house from a wholesaler. It is a duplex, and I paid $156,000. It needs about $20,000 in work and will be worth $220,000.

13. I bought this house from an agent who represented sellers that did not want to list on the MLS. I paid $85,000, and it is under contract to sell for $185,000. I put about $30,000 of work into it.

14. I bought this house from a wholesaler and paid $175,000. It needs $40,000 in work and will be worth $290,000.

15. I bought this house from the MLS for $170,000 and it will need $40,000 in work. It will be worth about $275,000.
16. I bought this house for $110,000 from the MLS and put $50,000 of work into it. It is under contract for almost $230,000.
17. I bought this house from the MLS for $155,000 and put $35,000 of work into it. It's under contract for about $250,000.
18. I bought this house from the foreclosure auction for $107,000. I put about $40,000 of work into it, and it is under contract to sell for more than $220,000.
19. I bought this house from a wholesaler for $56,000. We put an addition on it and will spend $80,000 on the rehab. It will be worth $200,000 when completed.
20. I bought this house for $130,000 from the MLS. It had a foundation issue, and with other repairs, we spent $45,000 on the remodel. We sold it for $244,000.

I bought all these houses in 2016 or 2017. I have a lot of flips going at once, so it takes me a while to repair them. I am in Northern Colorado, which has one of the hottest markets in the country. We have the lowest inventory we have ever had on the MLS, and I am still getting deals.

Making money on flips

As you can see from the above information, there is a lot of room between the sales price and the price I paid for the properties. There are many costs associated with a flip. There is also a lot of risk involved, as we saw in the case study I wrote about earlier. If there is not enough meat on the bone to make at least $25,000 on a flip, I do not buy the property because there is so much that can go wrong.

What is the Next Step?

This book lays the groundwork for how to make money flipping houses. You could take everything you learned and be successful. Don't let the naysayers keep you out of the game. Yes, you can lose money in real estate, but you can also make a lot of money. I flipped through the housing crisis and have known landlords who owned hundreds of rentals through the downturn with no issues. The people who lost money did not pay attention to the fundamentals and chased easy money.

If you invest the right way, flipping can change your life. Real estate changed my life by giving me a better way to invest, a better way to make money, and a better way to retire. Flipping has been a huge part of my success. Flipping is also exciting and tons of fun, although not as easy as TV makes it out to be.

As you know, I have a blog where I routinely write new articles and record podcasts. I encourage you to sign up for my email list if you want updates on everything I am doing as well as some other cool resources.

- You can sign up for my email list here: https://investfourmore.com/real-estate-investor-email-subscription/
- If you are interested in becoming an agent, I have a separate email list with more resources here: https://investfourmore.com/real-estate-agent-email-subscription/

I also have coaching programs available if you are interested in a little more help. I have video training courses and live courses where you can be on calls with me. These courses don't cost thousands and thousands of dollars either, like most you will find. You can find my courses on my resources page here:

https://investfourmore.com/resources

If you are interested in other types of investing I have additional paperback and Kindle best-selling books:

Build a Rental Property Empire: the no-nonsense book on finding deals, financing the right way, and managing wisely.

How to Buy a House: What Everyone Should Know Before They Buy or Sell a Home.

How to Change Your Mindset to Achieve Huge Success: Why your attitude and daily habits have more to do with making more money and having more freedom than anything else.

Fix and Flip Your Way to Financial Freedom Finding, Financing, Repairing and Selling Investment Properties.

The Book on Negotiating Real Estate: Expert Strategies for Getting the Best Deals When Buying & Selling Investment Property

How to Make it Big as a Real Estate Agent: The right systems and approaches to cut years off your learning curve and become successful in real estate.

I have made my books and coaching products as affordable as possible. I know people who are starting out in a new business do not have a lot of extra money. For those of you who know you need a little extra push and accountability, I created more in-depth training courses. These come with conference calls and email training with me personally. The Complete Blueprint for Successful Real Estate Investing is a rental property program that I created and comes with personal coaching from me as well as audio CDs/MP3s, videos, a huge how-to guide, and much more. If you are interested, send me an email, and I may have a special coupon for those that read this book all the way through! Mark@investfourmore.com.

I hope you enjoyed the book, and if you want to connect with me on social media check out the links below:

- Facebook
- LinkedIn
- Twitter
- Instagram
- Google +

About Mark Ferguson

I created Invest Four More to help people become real estate investors either as rental property owners, flippers, wholesalers, real estate agents, or even note owners. You may see pictures of me with my Lamborghini. It is a 1999 Lamborghini Diablo, which I bought in 2014. I had dreamed of owning a Lamborghini since I was a kid, and one of my public goals I wrote about in 2014 was buying one. It was an awesome experience setting that goal, being held accountable by my readers, and then accomplishing it. I even make sure I buy my cars below market value. I bought this car for $126,000, and it is worth about double that two years later.

The car is not a flashy marketing ploy but a reward for hard work. It signifies to me that we really can have what we want if we put our mind to it.

How did I get started?

I have been a licensed Realtor since 2001. My father has been a Realtor since 1978, and I was surrounded by real estate in my youth. I remember sleeping under my dad's desk when I was three while he worked tirelessly in the office. Surprisingly, or maybe not, I never wanted anything to do with real estate. I graduated from the University of Colorado in 2001 with a degree in business finance. I could not find a job that was appealing to me, so I reluctantly decided to work with my father part-time. Fifteen years later, I am sure glad I got into the real estate business!

Even though I had help getting started in real estate, I did not find success until I was five years into the business. I tried to follow my father's path, which did not mesh well with me. I found my own path as an REO agent, and my career took off. Many people think I had a huge advantage working with my father, and he was a great help, but I think that I actually would have been more successful sooner if I had been working on my own and was forced to find my own path.

Now, I run a real estate team of 10. My team sells 100 to 200 houses each year. I flip 10-15 houses per year, and I own 16 long-term rentals. I love real estate and investing in it because of the money I can make and the freedom running my own business brings. I also love big goals, and one of those goals is my plan to purchase 100 rental properties by January 2023.

I started Invest Four More in March 2013, and the primary objective was to provide information on investing in long-term rentals. I was not a writer until I started this blog. In fact, I had not written anything since college besides a basic letter. Readers who have been with me from the beginning may remember how tough it was to read my first articles with all the typos and poor grammar (I know it is still not perfect!). My goal has always been to provide incredible information, not to provide perfect articles with perfect grammar.

The name "InvestFourMore" is a play on words indicating that it is possible to finance more than four properties. The blog provides articles on financing, finding, buying, rehabbing, and renting out rental properties. The blog also discusses mortgage pay down strategies, fix and flips, advice for real estate agents, and many other real estate related topics.

I live in Greeley Colorado, which is about 50 miles north of Denver. I married my beautiful wife Jeni in 2008 and we have twins who turned five in June of 2016. When we met in 2005, Jeni was a Realtor but has since put her license on ice while she takes care of the twins. Jeni loves to sew and makes children's dresses under the label Kaiya Papaya.

Outside of work I love to travel, play golf, and work/play with my cars.

Made in the USA
Monee, IL
25 October 2020

45836525R00134